SUMMER MATH WORKBOOK

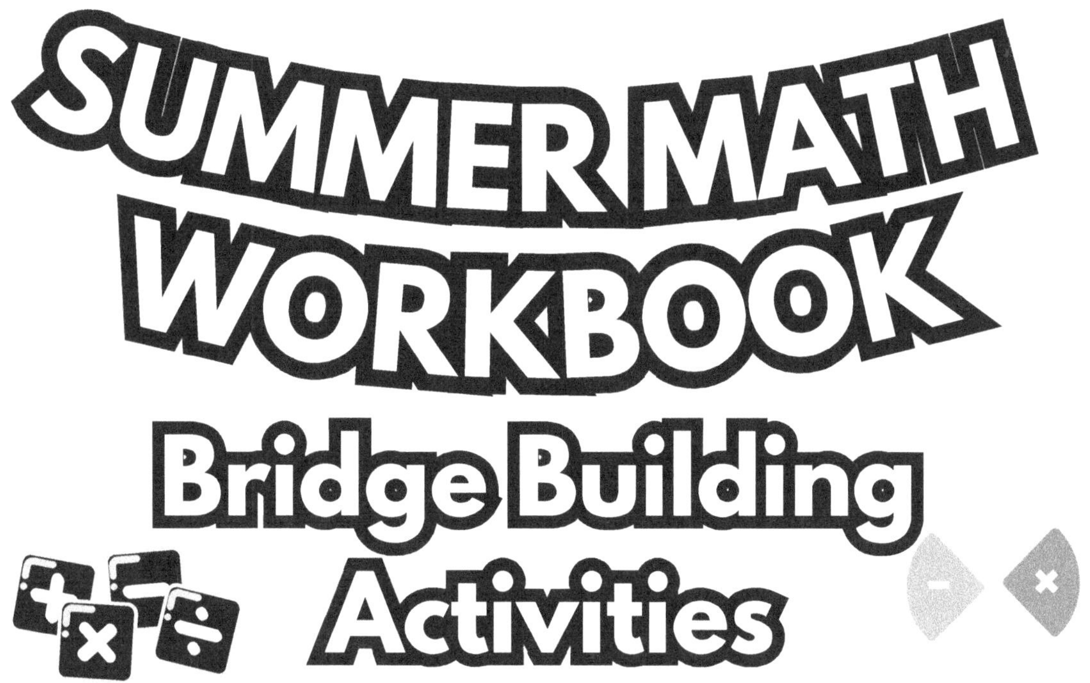

Introduction

As parents and educators, we understand the pivotal role that mathematics plays in shaping a child's academic journey and future success. Yet, the path to mathematical proficiency can often seem daunting, filled with challenges and complexities. That's where the transformative power of Summer Bridge Building Activities books comes into play, illuminating the way forward with clarity, precision, and purpose.

Summer vacation is a time for rest and relaxation, but it also presents the risk of the "summer slide," where students lose some of the academic gains they made during the school year. Summer Bridge Building Activities books are specifically designed to tackle this challenge, ensuring that your child stays academically engaged and prepared for the upcoming school year. These books provide a seamless bridge from one grade to the next, reinforcing essential skills and introducing new concepts that will give your child a head start.

Imagine your child eagerly diving into the pages of a Summer Bridge Building Activities book, greeted by clear, engaging content that demystifies complex mathematical concepts. With each turn of the pages, they embark on a journey of discovery, encountering thoughtfully curated practice questions that reinforce learning and sharpen problem-solving skills. As they unveil the answers to those questions, a sense of accomplishment blossoms within them — a tangible reward for their hard work and dedication.

Summer Bridge Building Activities books transcend traditional educational tools; they are meticulously crafted to build a deep and enduring understanding of mathematics. These books follow a sequential and logical progression, starting from fundamental principles and advancing to sophisticated problem-solving strategies. Each chapter is designed to build on the previous one, ensuring a solid and comprehensive foundation for future learning.

Parents, we yearn for nothing more than to see our children thrive academically and personally. We want to witness the spark of inspiration ignited within them as they overcome academic challenges with confidence and poise. Summer Bridge Building Activities books serve as indispensable partners in this noble endeavor, offering not just practice questions but the keys to unlocking a world of academic and personal opportunities.

Visualize the pride on your child's face as they master a challenging math concept, the joy they experience when their efforts yield results, and the confidence they gain with each success. These pages are designed to make learning math a positive, enriching, and deeply rewarding experience that will benefit them throughout their academic journey and beyond.

For educators, Summer Bridge Building Activities books are invaluable allies in the quest to cultivate mathematical proficiency in the classroom. Accompanied by comprehensive guides and readily available answers, instructors can focus on mentoring and nurturing their students, secure in the knowledge that these books provide a robust framework for effective learning.

Within the pages of Summer Bridge Building Activities books lies not just the promise of academic excellence, but the seeds of a brighter future. By integrating these resources into your child's summer routine, you are bestowing upon them the gifts of confidence, curiosity, and a lifelong love of learning.

Invest in your child's future today with Summer Bridge Building Activities books — because every great journey begins with a single step, and this step can change everything. Keep the momentum of learning alive over the summer, and watch your child soar to new academic heights.

Contents

Grade
1 2
SUMMER MATH
WORKBOOK
Bridge Building
Activities
Number Sense
Addition and Subtraction
Place Value

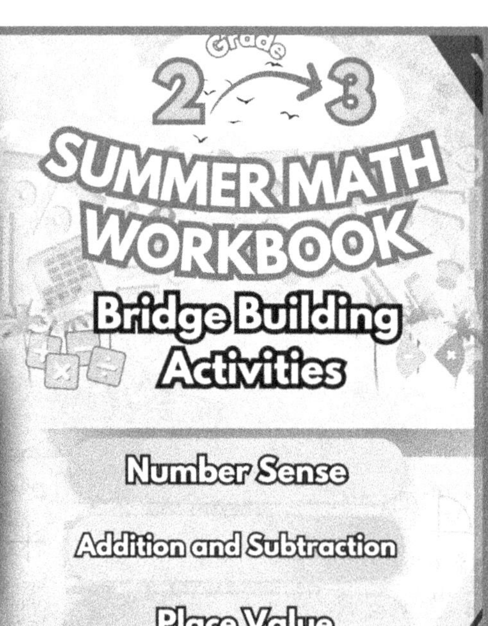
Grade
2 3
SUMMER MATH
WORKBOOK
Bridge Building
Activities
Number Sense
Addition and Subtraction
Place Value

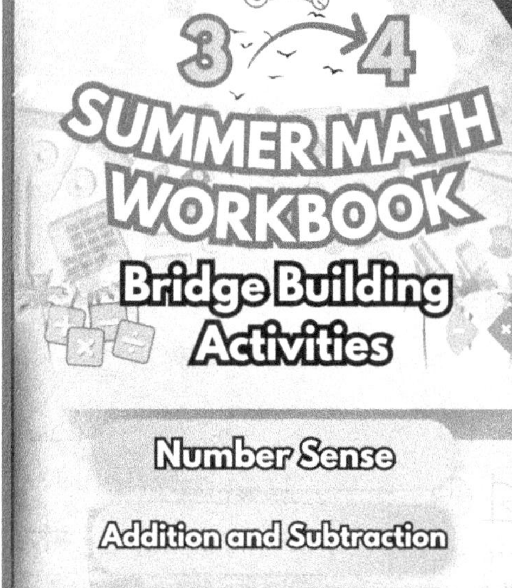
Grade
3 4
SUMMER MATH
WORKBOOK
Bridge Building
Activities
Number Sense
Addition and Subtraction
Place Value

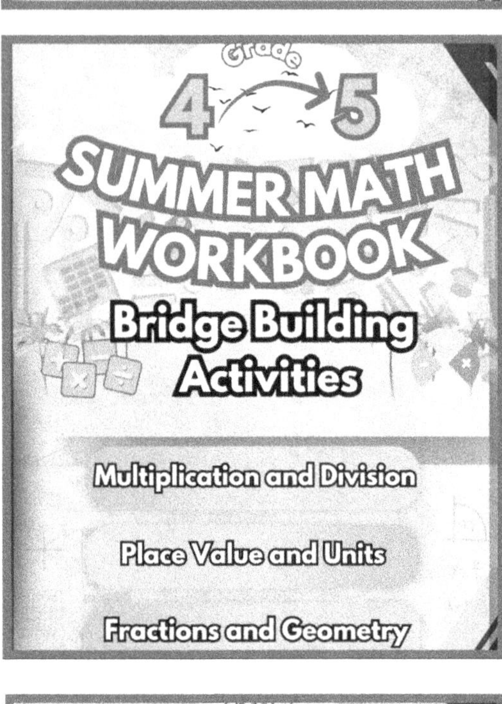
Grade
4 5
SUMMER MATH
WORKBOOK
Bridge Building
Activities
Multiplication and Division
Place Value and Units
Fractions and Geometry

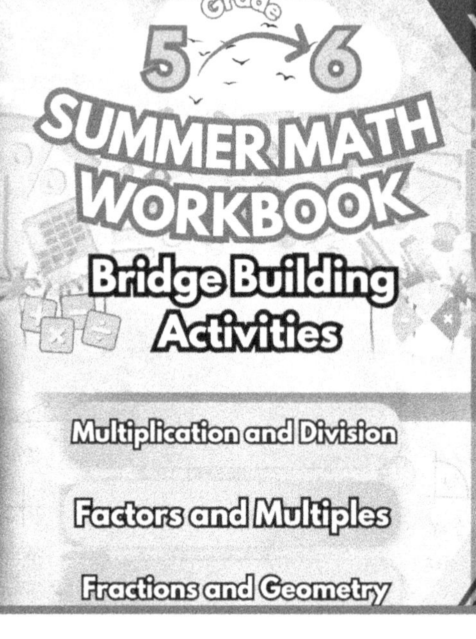
Grade
5 6
SUMMER MATH
WORKBOOK
Bridge Building
Activities
Multiplication and Division
Factors and Multiples
Fractions and Geometry

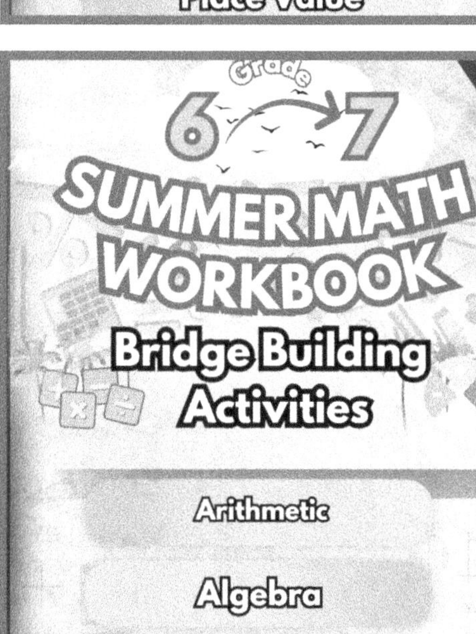
Grade
6 7
SUMMER MATH
WORKBOOK
Bridge Building
Activities
Arithmetic
Algebra
Geometry and Statistics

Grade
7 8
SUMMER MATH
WORKBOOK
Bridge Building
Activities
Ratio and Percentage
Algebra and Cartesian Plane
Geometry and Statistics

Grade
8 9
SUMMER MATH
WORKBOOK
Bridge Building
Activities
Ratio and Percentage
Algebra
Geometry and Graphing

Grade
9 10
SUMMER MATH
WORKBOOK
Bridge Building
Activities
Factoring and Distributing
Algebra
Geometry and Graphing

Foundations of Arithmetic

Positive and negative integers are whole numbers that can represent quantities greater than zero and less than zero, respectively.

Positive Integers: Positive integers are whole numbers greater than zero. They are denoted by the numbers 1,2,3,4...

Negative Integers: Negative integers are whole numbers less than zero. They are denoted by placing a negative sign ("-") before the numbers, such as $-1,-2,-3,-4,...$

The positive integers are used to represent the number of objects, scores, etc. whereas the negative integers can be used to represent debt, losses, temperatures below freezing points, etc.

Let's solve some problems:

1. 6 – (– 8) – 9

- Start by simplifying within the parentheses:

  $-(-8)$ becomes 8.

- Rewrite the expression with the simplified part:

  $6 + 8 - 9.$

- Now perform addition and subtraction from left to right:

  $6 + 8 = 1\ 4$, then $14 - 9 = 5$

2. (– 5) – (– 3) + 10

$(-5) + 3 + 10$

$(-5) + 3 = -2$, then $-2 + 10 = 8$

<u>**Exponents**</u>

An exponent tells you how many times a number (called the base) is multiplied by itself. It is written as a superscript to the right of the base number. For example, in 2^3, 2 is the base and 3 is the exponent.

Rules:

1. **Product Rule**: When multiplying powers with the same base, add the exponents.

$$a^m \times a^n = a^{m+n}$$

For example:

$$2^3 = 2 \times 2 \times 2 = 8$$

$$3^2 \times 3^4 = 3^{2+4} = 3^6 = 3 \times 3 \times 3 \times 3 \times 3 \times 3 = 729$$

2. **Quotient Rule**: When dividing powers with the same base, subtract the exponents.

$$a^m \div a^n = a^{m-n}$$

For example:

$$5^3 \div 5^2 = 5^{3-2} = 5^1 = 5$$

3. **Power of a Power Rule**: When raising a power to another power, multiply the exponents.

$$(a^m)^n = a^{mn}$$

For example:

$$(2^2)^3 = 2^{2 \times 3} = 26 = 64$$

4. **Power of a Product Rule**: When raising a product to a power, distribute the power to each factor.

$$(ab)^n = a^n \times b^n$$

For example:

$$(2 \times 3)^2 = 2^2 \times 3^2 = 4 \times 9 = 36$$

5. **Power of a Quotient Rule**: When raising a quotient to a power, distribute the power to the numerator and denominator separately.

$$\left(\frac{a}{b}\right)^n = \frac{a^n}{b^n}$$

For example:

$$\left(\frac{4}{2}\right)^3 = \frac{4^3}{2^3} = \frac{64}{8} = 8$$

6. **Zero Exponent Rule**: Any nonzero number raised to the power of zero equals 11.

$$a^0 = 1$$

For example:

$$7^0 = 1$$

7. **Negative Exponent Rule**: A negative exponent means the reciprocal of the base raised to the positive exponent.

$$a^{-n} = \frac{1}{a^n}$$

For example:

$$2^{-3} = \frac{1}{2^3} = \frac{1}{8}$$

To evaluate expressions with exponents, we can use:

- **Repeated Multiplication**: Perform the multiplication indicated by the exponent.

- **Using the Rules of Exponents**: Apply the appropriate rule to simplify expressions involving exponents.

Square Roots

The square root of a number is a value that, when multiplied by itself, gives the original number. It's denoted by the symbol $\sqrt{\ }$.

For example, the square root of 9 is 3 because 3 * 3 = 9.

Cube Roots

The cube root of a number is a value that, when multiplied by itself twice, gives the original number. It's denoted by the symbol $\sqrt[3]{\ }$.

For example, the cube root of 8 is 2 because 2 * 2 * 2 = 8.

Factors

Factors are numbers that divide another number without leaving a remainder.

For example, the factors of 12 are 1, 2, 3, 4, 6, and 12 because these numbers can divide 12 evenly.

Factors always come in pairs, except for perfect squares.

Multiples

Multiples are the result of multiplying a number by an integer.

For example, the multiples of 3 are 3, 6, 9, 12, 15, and so on because these numbers are obtained by multiplying 3 by 1, 2, 3, 4, 5, and so on.

Every number has an infinite number of multiples.

Every factor of a number is a divisor of that number, and every multiple of a number is divisible by that number.

Let's solve some problems:

Factors of **44**

2, 4, 11, 22

Multiples of **77**

77, 154, 231, 308, 385

Pre-Algebra

Order of Operations (PEMDAS)

The order of operations, often remembered by the acronym PEMDAS, stands for:

- **Parentheses**: Perform operations inside parentheses first.
- **Exponents**: Evaluate exponents (powers and roots) next.
- **Multiplication and Division**: Perform multiplication and division from left to right.
- **Addition and Subtraction:** Perform addition and subtraction from left to right.

The order of operations helps to clarify which operations should be performed first in a mathematical expression to ensure consistent and accurate results.

- **Parentheses**: Evaluate expressions within parentheses first. If there are nested parentheses, start with the innermost ones and work your way out.

    1. Example: $2 \times (3 + 4) = 2 \times 7 = 14$

- **Exponents**: Evaluate expressions with exponents (powers and roots) next.

    1. Example: $2^3 + 4 = 8 + 4 = 12$

- **Multiplication and Division**: Perform multiplication and division from left to right.

    1. Example: $2 \times 3 + 4 = 6 + 4 = 10$

2. Example: $6 \div 2 \times 3 = 3 \times 3 = 9$

- **Addition and Subtraction**: Perform addition and subtraction from left to right.

    1. Example: $2 + 3 \times 4 = 2 + 12 = 14$

    2. Example: $10 - 4 \div 2 = 10 - 2 = 8$

Solving Equations (One Step)

Solving one-step equations involves performing a single operation to isolate the variable and find its value.

Let's solve an equation step by step: $16 + x = 31$

1. **Identify the Goal**:

    The goal is to isolate the variable x on one side of the equation.

2. **Simplify the Equation**: Combine like terms on both sides of the equation, if necessary.

    The equation is already simplified.

3. **Undo Addition or Subtraction**: If there's addition or subtraction involving the variable, undo it by performing the opposite operation on both sides of the equation.

    Since x is being added to 16, we'll undo this operation by subtracting 16 from both sides of the equation:
    $$16 + x - 16 = 31 - 16$$

4. **Isolate the Variable**: Ensure that the variable is alone on one side of the equation.

$$x = 15$$

5. **Check Your Solution**: Substitute the value of x back into the original equation to verify that it satisfies the equation.

$$16 + 15 = 31$$

$$31 = 31$$

The equation is balanced, so the solution.

Evaluate Expressions

Evaluating expressions involves substituting given values for variables in an expression and then performing the indicated operations to find the result.

For example: Let's evaluate $4x - 10$, when $x = 3$:

Step 1: Substitute the given value for the variable:

Replace every occurrence of x in the expression $4x - 10$ with the given value, which is 3:

$$= 4(3) - 10$$

Step 2: Perform the operations:

Perform the indicated operations according to the order of operations (PEMDAS - Parentheses, Exponents, Multiplication and Division, Addition and Subtraction):

$$= 4 \times 3 - 10$$

Step 3: Simplify:

Calculate the result:

$$12 - 10 = 2$$

Solving Inequalities

Inequalities are mathematical expressions that compare the relative sizes of two values. They are used to express relationships where one quantity is:

- "$<$" (less than),
- "$>$" (greater than),
- "$<=$" (less than or equal to),
- "$>=$" (greater than or equal to),
- and "$\neq$" (not equal to) another quantity.

For example:

$$y + -10 \leq -8$$

To isolate y, we need to get rid of the constant term -10. Since -10 is being subtracted from y, we can undo this operation by adding 10 to both sides of the inequality:

$$y - 10 + 10 \leq -8 + 10$$

$$y \leq 2$$

To check the solution:

$$2 - 10 \leq -8$$

$$-8 = -8$$

The inequality is true when $y = 2$

Ratio and Proportion

A proportional relationship between two quantities exists when they have a constant ratio or when one is a multiple of the other. In other words, if we increase one quantity, the other quantity will increase or decrease by the same factor. For example, if we double one quantity, the other quantity will also double.

Let's solve a problem:

$$\frac{\square}{9} = \frac{8}{18}$$

Step 1: Cross Multiply: Cross multiply by multiplying the numerator of one fraction by the denominator of the other, and vice versa:

$$x \times 18 = 9 \times 8$$

Step 2: Solve for the Unknown: Perform the multiplication on both sides of the equation:

$$18x = 72$$

Step 3: Divide Both Sides by the Coefficient of the Unknown: To isolate x, divide both sides of the equation by the coefficient of x, which is 18:

$$\frac{18x}{18} = \frac{72}{18}$$

$$x = 4$$

Step 4: Verify Check your solution by substituting $x = 4$ back into the original equation:

$$\frac{4}{9} = \frac{8}{18}$$

Since both sides are equal, the solution x = 4 is correct.

Percentage

Percentage is a way of expressing a number as a fraction of 100. It is commonly used to represent proportions, rates, and comparisons. The symbol "%" is used to denote percentages.

To calculate a percentage, we multiply the given number by the appropriate fraction or decimal equivalent.

How to calculate a percentage:

Convert Percentage to Decimal: If the percentage is given as a percentage value (e.g., 25%), convert it to its decimal equivalent by dividing by 100.

For example, 25% as a decimal is $\frac{25}{100}$ = 0.25

Multiply: Multiply the decimal equivalent of the percentage by the given number. This gives us the portion of the number that represents the percentage.

$$100 \text{ x } 0.25 = 25\%$$

Result: The result is the calculated percentage value.

For example, to calculate 25% of 80:

Convert 25% to a decimal: 25% = 0.25.

Multiply 0.25 by 80: 0.25 × 80 = 20. The result is 20.

<h1 style="text-align:center"><u>Geometry</u></h1>

<u>Area and Perimeter</u>

The area of a shape represents the amount of space it occupies. The perimeter of a shape is the total distance around its outer edge.

Area of Rectangle

For a square, since all four sides are equal, we only need to know the length of one side to find its area. We can calculate the area of a square by multiplying the length of one side by itself (squared). So, if the length of one side of the square is 's', then the area (A) is given by:

$$A = s \times s$$

4 in

4 in

$$A = 4 \times 4$$

$$A = 16$$

Perimeter of Rectangle

For a square, since all four sides are equal, we can find the perimeter by adding up the lengths of all four sides. If 's' represents the length of one side, then the perimeter (P) is given by:

$$P = 4 \times s$$

$$P = 4 \times 4$$

$$P = 16$$

Area of Triangle:

The area of a triangle represents the amount of space enclosed within its three sides. The formula for calculating the area of a triangle depends on the type of triangle. For a general triangle, we use the formula:

$$A = \frac{1}{2} \times base \times height$$

Where:

- *A* represents the area of the triangle.

- The base is the length of any one side of the triangle.

- The height is the perpendicular distance from the base to the opposite vertex.

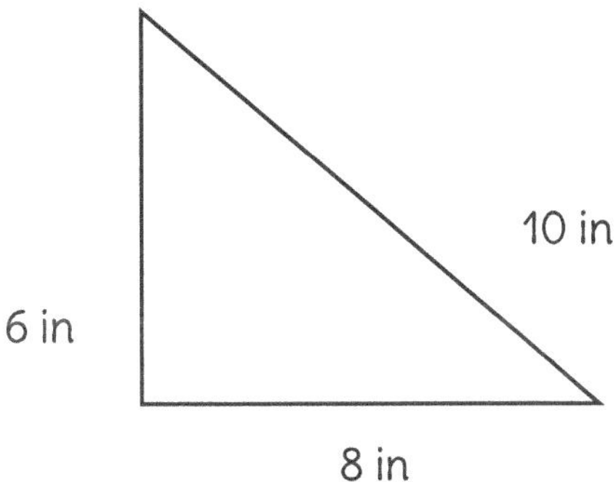

$$A = \frac{1}{2} \times \text{base} \times \text{height}$$

$$A = \frac{1}{2} \times 6 \times 8$$

$$A = \frac{1}{2} \times 48$$

$$A = 24$$

Perimeter of Triangle:

The perimeter of a triangle is the total length of its three sides. To find the perimeter, we simply add the lengths of all three sides together:

$$P = \text{side1} + \text{side2} + \text{side3}$$

$$P = 6 + 8 + 10$$

$$P = 24$$

Equilateral Triangle

An equilateral triangle is a triangle in which all three sides are equal in length. To find the area and perimeter of an equilateral triangle, we can use the following formulas:

- Area (A): $\frac{\sqrt{3}}{4} \times a^2$ where a is the length of one side of the equilateral triangle.
- Perimeter (P): $P = 3a$ where a is the length of one side of the equilateral triangle.

Area of Equilateral Triangle:

$$\text{Area (A): } \frac{\sqrt{3}}{4} \times (6)^2$$

$$\text{Area (A): } \frac{\sqrt{3}}{4} \times 36$$

$$\text{Area (A): } \frac{36\sqrt{3}}{4}$$

$$\text{Area (A): } \frac{36(1.73)}{4}$$

$$\text{Area (A): } \frac{62.35}{4}$$

$$\text{Area (A): } 15.59 \text{ in}^2$$

Perimeter of Equilateral Triangle:

$$P = 3a$$

$$P = 3(6) = 18$$

Isosceles Triangle

An isosceles triangle is a triangle with at least two sides of equal length. The angles opposite the equal sides are also equal.

Area of Isosceles Triangle

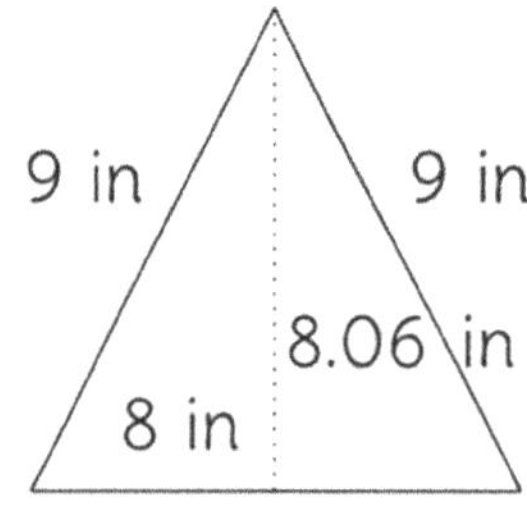

$$A = \frac{1}{2} \times \text{base} \times \text{height}$$

$$A = \frac{1}{2} \times 8 \times 8$$

$$A = \frac{1}{2} \times 64$$

$$A = 32$$

Perimeter of Isosceles Triangle

The perimeter of a triangle is the total length of its three sides. To find the perimeter, we simply add the lengths of all three sides together:

$$P = \text{side1} + \text{side2} + \text{side3}$$

$$P = 9 + 9 + 8$$

$$P = 26$$

Scalene Triangle

A scalene triangle is a triangle with no equal sides and no equal angles. The formula for finding various properties of a scalene triangle is as follows:

Area (A): The area of a scalene triangle can be calculated using Heron's fo rmula, which is given by:

$$A = \sqrt{s(s-a)(s-b)(s-c)}$$

where s is the semi-perimeter of the triangle,

and a, b, and c are the lengths of its three sides.

Perimeter (P): The perimeter of a scalene triangle is the sum of the lengths of its three sides.

$$P = side1 + side2 + side3$$

Let's find the Area and Perimeter of a Scalene Triangle:

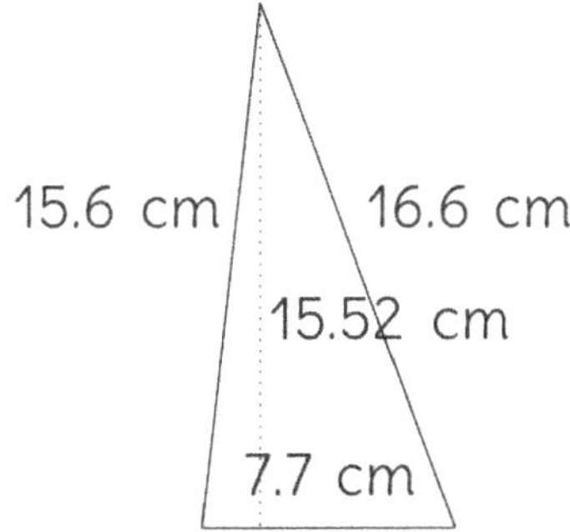

Area (A): First, we calculate the semi-perimeter (s):

$$S = \frac{a+b+c}{2} = \frac{15.6 + 16.6 + 7.7}{2} = \frac{39.8}{2} = 19.9 \text{ cm}$$

Heron's formula to find the area:

$$A = \sqrt{s(s-a)(s-b)(s-c)}$$

$$A = \sqrt{19.9(19.9-15.6)(19.9-16.6)(19.9-7.7)}$$

$$A = \sqrt{19.9 \times 4.3 \times 3.3 \times 12.2}$$

$$A = \sqrt{3445} \approx 59$$

Perimeter (P):

$$P = \text{side1} + \text{side2} + \text{side3}$$

$$P = 15.6 + 16.6 + 7.7$$

$$P = 39.8$$

Area and Perimeter of an L-shape

The L-shaped figure typically consists of two rectangles joined together to form an L-shape. To find the area and perimeter of an L-shaped figure, we will need to calculate the areas and perimeters of each rectangle and then combine them.

Area=Area of Rectangle 1 + Area of Rectangle 2

Perimeter=Perimeter of Rectangle 1 + Perimeter of Rectangle 2

Let's find the Area and Perimeter of an L-shape:

10.92 cm

4.38 cm

11.28 cm

6.78 cm

Area of L-Shape

$$\text{Area 1} = 4.38 \times 4.5 = 19.7 \text{ cm}^2$$

$$\text{Area 2} = 11.28 \times 6.54 = 73.7 \text{ cm}^2$$

$$\text{Area} = 19.7 + 73.7$$

$$\text{Area} = 93.481 \text{ cm}^2$$

Perimeter of L-Shape

$$P = 11.28 + 6.54 + 6.78 + 4.38 + 4.5 + 10.92$$

$$P = 44.4 \text{ cm}$$

<u>Area and Perimeter of U-shape</u>

U-shape is basically composed of three rectangles, we'll need to calculate the area and perimeter of each rectangle separately and then sum them up.

Area of the U-shape:

The total area (A) of the U-shape is the sum of the areas of the three rectangles:

$$A = A1 + A2 + A3$$

Perimeter of the U-shape: The total perimeter (P) of the U-shape is the sum of the perimeters of the three rectangles:

$$P = P1 + P2 + P3$$

Let's find the area and perimeter of the following U-shape:

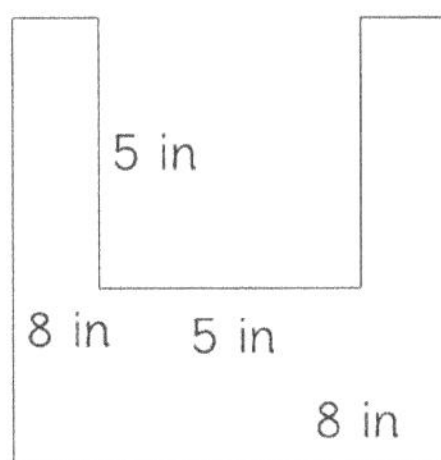

Area:

$$A1 = 8 \times 1.5 = 12 + A2 = 3 \times 5 = 15 + A3 = 8 \times 1.5 = 12$$

$$= 12 + 15 + 12$$

$$= 39 \text{ in}^2$$

Perimeter:

$$2 \times 8 + 2 \times 5 + 2 \times 8$$

$$= 16 + 10 + 16$$

$$= 42$$

Area and Circumference of circles

To find the area (A) and circumference (C) of a circle, we use the following formulas:

1. **Area of a Circle (A)** $= \pi \times (radius)^2$
   - where π (pi) is a constant with value of (3.14). It is a ratio of the circumference of a circle to its diameter,
   - the radius (r) is the distance from the center of the circle.
2. **Circumference of a Circle (C)** $= 2 \times \pi \times radius$

Let's solve an example: suppose a swimming pool has a radius of 11 meters, we are required to calculate its Area and Circumference:

$$\textbf{Area } \textbf{\textit{(A)}} = \pi \times (radius)^2$$

$$\textbf{\textit{A}} = 3.14 \times 11^2$$

$$\textbf{\textit{A}} = 3.14 \times 121$$

$$\textbf{\textit{A}} = 379.94 \text{ square meters}$$

$$\textbf{Circumference } \textbf{\textit{(C)}} = 2 \times \pi \times radius$$

$$\textbf{\textit{C}} = 2 \times 3.14 \times 11$$

$$\textbf{\textit{C}} = 69.08 \text{ square meters}$$

<u>**Angles**</u>

Types of Angles: Angles can be classified based on their measures:

- **Acute Angle:** An angle less than 90°.

- **Right Angle:** An angle exactly equal to 90°.

- **Obtuse Angle:** An angle greater than 90° and less than 180°.

- **Straight Angle:** An angle exactly equal to 180°.

- **Reflex Angle:** An angle greater than 180° and less than 360°.

- **Full Angle:** An angle equal to 360°.

Measure angles with a protractor. It looks like a semicircle or a half-disc with degree markings from 0° to 180°.To measure an angle using a protractor, we place the center of the protractor at the vertex of the angle, align one side of the angle with the zero mark on the protractor, and read the degree measure where the other side intersects the protractor.

For example, let's measure the following angle.

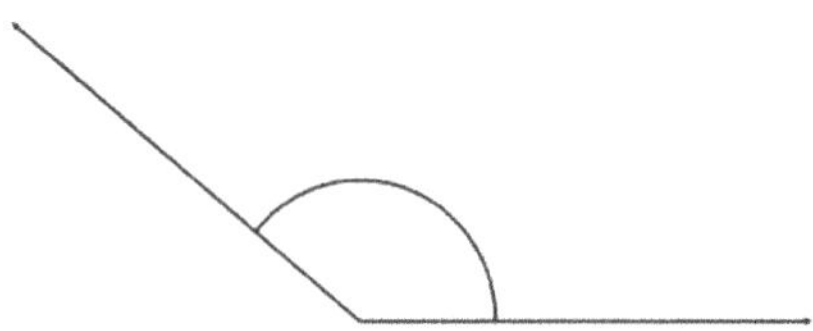

The angle is 140°.

We also know that the angle is greater than 90° and less than 180°, so this is an Obtuse angle.

Volume and surface Area

Volume refers to the amount of space occupied by a three-dimensional object. For shapes like cubes or rectangular prisms, we calculate volume by multiplying their length, width, and height.

To find the volume V of a rectangular prism, we use the formula:

$$Volume \ = \ length \ x \ width \ x \ height$$

Surface Area represents the total area covering all the faces of a three-dimensional object. For shapes like cubes or rectangular prisms, we find the surface area by summing the areas of all its faces.

The formula for surface area SA of a cube or rectangular prism is:

$$Surface \ Area \ = \ 2lw \ + \ 2lh \ + \ 2wh$$

Where: l is the length, w is the width, and h is the height of the object.

For example: Let's find the Volume and Surface Area of following rectangular prisms:

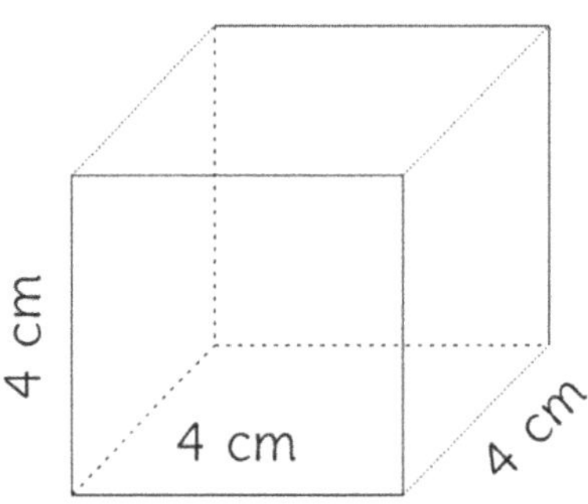

$$Volume \ = \ length \ \times \ width \ \times \ height$$

$$= 4 \times 4 \times 4$$

$$= 64 \text{ cm}^2$$

$$Surface\ Area = 2lw + 2lh + 2wh$$

$$= 2(4 \times 4) + 2(4 \times 4) + 2(4 \times 4)$$

$$= 32 + 32 + 32$$

$$= 96 \text{ cm2}$$

Different 3D objects have unique formulas for finding their volume and surface area. Here are some common ones:

1. Cube:

- Volume: $V = s^3$ (where s is the length of one side of the cube)

- Surface area: $SA = 6s^2$

2. Sphere:

- Volume: $V = (\frac{4}{3})\pi r^3$ (where r is the radius of the sphere)

- Surface area: $SA = 4\pi r^2$

3. Cone:

- Volume: $V = (\frac{1}{3})\pi r^2 h$ (where r is the radius of the base and h is the height of the cone)

- Surface area: $SA = \pi r^2 + \pi r \sqrt{(r^2 + h^2)}$

4. Cylinder:

- Volume: $V = \pi r^2 h$ (where r is the radius of the base and h is the height of the cylinder)

- Surface area: $SA = 2\pi r^2 + 2\pi rh$

5. Pyramid:

- Volume: $V = \left(\frac{1}{3}\right)Bh$ (where B is the area of the base and h is the height of the pyramid)

- Surface area: $SA = B + \frac{1}{2}Pl$ (where P is the perimeter of the base and l is the slant height of the pyramid)

<u>Statistics</u>

<u>Mean</u>

The mean, also known as the average, is a measure of central tendency.

To find the mean of a set of numbers:

- Add up all the numbers in the set.
- Divide the sum by the total count of numbers in the set.

For example: consider the set of numbers: 70, 72, 49, 69, 27, 76.

$$\text{Mean} = \frac{70 + 72 + 49 + 69 + 27 + 76}{6} = \frac{363}{6} = 60.5$$

<u>Median</u>

The median is a measure of central tendency that represents the middle value of a dataset when the values are arranged in ascending or descending order.

To find the median of a set of numbers:

- Arrange the numbers in ascending or descending order.
- If the total count of numbers is odd, the median is the middle value.
- If the total count of numbers is even, the median is the average of the two middle values.

For example: consider the set of numbers: 70, 72, 49, 69, 27, 76.

$$27, 49, 69, 70, 72, 76$$

$$\text{Median} = \frac{69 + 70}{2} = \frac{139}{2} = 69.5$$

<u>Mode:</u>

The mode in statistics refers to the value that appears most frequently in a given set of data.

Let's consider the following set of numbers:

$$\{2, 4, 4, 5, 6, 6, 6, 7, 8, 8\}$$

In this set, the number 6 appears three times, more than any other number. Therefore, the mode of this dataset is 6.

It's possible for a dataset to have more than one mode if two or more numbers appear with the same highest frequency. In such cases, the dataset is considered multimodal. If no number repeats, the dataset is considered to have no mode.

For example:

$$\{2, 4, 4, 4, 5, 6, 6, 6, 7, 8, 8\}$$

In this date set, 4 and 6 appear three times. Therefore, this dataset is multimodal.

<u>Range:</u>

In statistics, the range refers to the difference between the largest and smallest values in a dataset. It represents the spread or variability of the data.

For example, consider the dataset { 68, 13, 30, 18, 45, 76, 11}:

To calculate the range:

1. Arrange the data points in ascending order.

$$11, 13, 18, 30, 45, 68, 76$$

2. Subtract the smallest value from the largest value.

- The smallest value is 11.
- The largest value is 76.

$$\text{Range} = \text{Largest value - smallest value} = 76 - 11 = 65.$$

Exponents

Convert the values.

1. $5^2 =$ _______________

2. $10^{-2} =$ _______________

3. $13^{-2} =$ _______________

4. $19^{-2} =$ _______________

5. $9^3 =$ _______________

6. $3^3 =$ _______________

7. $11^{-2} =$ _______________

8. $6^4 =$ _______________

9. $16^3 =$ _______________

10. $15^3 =$ _______________

11. $16^{-2} =$ ___________________

12. $14^3 =$ ___________________

13. $5^{-2} =$ ___________________

14. $4^2 =$ ___________________

15. $6^{-2} =$ ___________________

16. $20^{-3} =$ ___________________

17. $12^{-2} =$ ___________________

18. $8^4 =$ ___________________

19. $6^{-3} =$ ___________________

20. $9^4 =$ ___________________

21. $17^{-3} =$ ______________________

22. $7^{3} =$ ______________________

23. $4^{-2} =$ ______________________

24. $19^{-3} =$ ______________________

25. $13^{3} =$ ______________________

26. $6^{2} =$ ______________________

27. $9^{2} =$ ______________________

28. $20^{2} =$ ______________________

29. $18^{3} =$ ______________________

30. $19^{2} =$ ______________________

Square and Cube Roots

Calculate the root of each value.

1. $\sqrt[3]{2,197} =$ _______________

2. $\sqrt[3]{1} =$ _______________

3. $\sqrt[3]{216} =$ _______________

4. $\sqrt{961} =$ _______________

5. $\sqrt[3]{27} =$ _______________

6. $\sqrt[3]{1,728} =$ _______________

7. $\sqrt[3]{1,000} =$ _______________

8. $\sqrt[3]{125} =$ _______________

9. $\sqrt[3]{512} =$ _______________

10. $\sqrt{25} =$ _______________

11. $\sqrt{1,024} =$ _______________

12. $\sqrt{289} =$ _______________

13. $\sqrt[3]{64} =$ _______________

14. $\sqrt{1} =$ _______________

15. $\sqrt{64} =$ _______________

16. $\sqrt[3]{10,648} =$ _______________

17. $\sqrt[3]{2,744} =$ _______________

18. $\sqrt{441} =$ _______________

19. $\sqrt[3]{8} =$ _______________

20. $\sqrt[3]{729} =$ _______________

21. $\sqrt{144} =$ _______________

22. $\sqrt{4} =$ _______________

23. $\sqrt{529} =$ _______________

24. $\sqrt[3]{3,375} =$ _______________

25. $\sqrt{49} =$ _______________

26. $\sqrt[3]{6{,}859} =$ _______________

27. $\sqrt[3]{8{,}000} =$ _______________

28. $\sqrt[3]{343} =$ _______________

29. $\sqrt[3]{4{,}096} =$ _______________

30. $\sqrt{784} =$ _______________

31. $\sqrt{625} =$ _______________

32. $\sqrt{2{,}116} =$ _______________

33. $\sqrt{576} =$ _______________

34. $\sqrt{3{,}969} =$ _______________

35. $\sqrt{100} =$ _______________

36. $\sqrt{81} =$ _______________

Factors

1. 8
   ____

2. 33
   ____

3. 12
   ____

4. 10
   ____

5. 5
   ____

6. 93
   ____

7. 30
   ____

8. 1

____

9. 23

____

10. 21

____

11. 6

____

12. 38

____

13. 77

____

14. 7

____

15. 63 ____

16. 31 ____

17. 11 ____

18. 83 ____

19. 4 ____

20. 25 ____

21. 76 ____

22. 27 ______________________________

23. 47 ______________________________

24. 29 ______________________________

25. 65 ______________________________

26. 58 ______________________________

27. 89 ______________________________

28. 64 ______________________________

Multiples

1. 11
   ____

2. 31
   ____

3. 3
   ____

4. 5
   ____

5. 6
   ____

6. 9
   ____

7. 94
   ____

8. 46 ___________________________

9. 4 ___________________________

10. 59 ___________________________

11. 2 ___________________________

12. 8 ___________________________

13. 100 ___________________________

14. 65 ___________________________

15. 75 _______________

16. 26 _______________

17. 69 _______________

18. 56 _______________

19. 93 _______________

20. 73 _______________

21. 60 _______________

22. 80 ____

23. 96 ____

24. 43 ____

25. 44 ____

26. 52 ____

27. 1 ____

28. 71 ____

Positive and Negative Integers

Evaluate.

1. $3 + 1 + 1 + 10 =$

2. $3 + 9 + 8 =$

3. $5 + 9 + 10 + 2 =$

4. $2 + 6 + 7 + 10 =$

5. $6 + 8 + 1 + 2 =$

6. $4 + 4 + 6 + 7 =$

7. $9 + 1 + 7 + 4 =$

8. $4 + 1 + 3 =$

9. $3 + 10 + 7 =$

10. $9 + 4 + 4 + 4 =$

11. $6 + 4 + 7 =$

12. $9 + 8 + 2 + 7 =$

13. $1 + 8 + 5 =$

14. $1 + 7 + 9 + 3 =$

15. $5 + 4 + 7 =$

16. $1 + 7 + 4 =$

17. $3 + 9 + 6 + 5 =$

18. $4 + 5 + 7 + 8 =$

19. $2 + 5 + 7 =$

20. $3 + 6 + 3 + 2 =$

21. $8 + 6 + 6 =$

22. $6 + 5 + 1 =$

23. $8 + 4 + 3 + 4 =$

24. $7 + 3 + 1 =$

25. $9 + 7 + 1 + 8 =$

26. $7 + 1 + 1 + 7 =$

27. $8 + 2 + 5 + 4 =$

28. $5 + 9 + 10 + 3 =$

29. $8 + 8 + 2 =$

30. $6 + 1 + 7 + 8 =$

31. $2 + 5 + 3 + 4 =$

32. $5 + 6 + 4 =$

33. $1 + 8 + 2 + 7 =$

34. $10 + 5 + 5 =$

SUMMER MATH WORKBOOK

BUILDING ACTIVITIES

Order of Operations (PEMDAS)

Evaluate Expressions.

1. $8 + 2 + 9 + 10 =$

2. $5 + 9 + 9 + 2 =$

3. $6 + 5 + 7 + 8 =$

4. $5 + 2 + 2 =$

5. $3 + 2 + 7 =$

6. $6 + 9 + 5 + 2 =$

7. $5 + 7 + 9 =$

8. $6 + 5 + 6 =$

9. $3 + 9 + 6 =$

10. $4 + 6 + 3 + 3 =$

11. $2 + 2 + 3 =$

12. $4 + 2 + 6 + 6 =$

13. $1 + 3 + 4 =$

14. $4 + 6 + 9 =$

15. $2 + 2 + 6 + 10 =$

16. $7 + 6 + 7 + 7 =$

17. $7 + 3 + 1 + 10 =$

18. $5 + 4 + 9 + 7 =$

19. $9 + 4 + 2 =$

20. $2 + 9 + 1 + 1 =$

21. $10 + 3 + 4 + 3 =$

22. $9 + 1 + 3 =$

23. $4 + 5 + 1 =$

24. $7 + 5 + 1 + 4 =$

25. $7 + 7 + 1 + 6 =$

26. $7 + 5 + 10 =$

27. $2 + 5 + 8 =$

28. $3 + 7 + 4 =$

Solving Equations: (One Side)

Solve the equations for the variable.

1. $5 = x \div 1$

2. $2 + x = 13$

3. $27 = 16 + x$

4. $288 = 18 \times x$

5. $13 = x \div 5$

6. $13 = 39 \div x$

7. $x \div 6 = 15$

8. $3 = 20 - x$

9. $18 = x - 2$

10. $x \times 20 = 140$

11. $10 = x + 8$

12. $20 = 280 \div x$

13. $28 = 11 + x$

14. $3 = x \div 4$

15. $36 = 6 \times x$

16. $x + 14 = 16$

17. $150 = 15 \times x$

18. $15 = x - 5$

19. $1 = x - 3$

20. $12 = 15 - x$

21. $x - 9 = 9$

22. $2 = 4 \div x$

23. $9 = 4 + x$

24. $13 = x \div 2$

25. $5 = 13 - x$

26. $247 = 19 \times x$

27. $11 - x = 8$

28. $x + 15 = 29$

Evaluate Expressions

Evaluate the expression when: $x = 1$

1. $x - 8 =$

2. $8 - x =$

3. $6 + x =$

4. $x - 1 =$

5. $x + 9 =$

6. $8 + x =$

7. $x - 9 =$

8. $4 - x =$

Evaluate Expressions

Evaluate the expression when: $x = 4$

1. $7 + x =$

2. $3 - x =$

3. $9 - x =$

4. $10 + x =$

5. $7 - x =$

6. $x - 3 =$

7. $1 - x =$

8. $x + 5 =$

Evaluate Expressions

Evaluate the expression when: $x = 1$

1. $x - 5 =$

2. $x - 8 =$

3. $x - 9 =$

4. $6 - x =$

5. $5 - x =$

6. $x - 1 =$

7. $x - 3 =$

8. $10 + x =$

Evaluate Expressions

Evaluate the expression when: $x = 3$

1. $9 + x =$

2. $2 - x =$

3. $x - 4 =$

4. $x - 3 =$

5. $x + 2 =$

6. $x + 8 =$

7. $6 - x =$

8. $x - 5 =$

One-Step Equations

Solve for the variable.

1. $6 = 1 + y$

2. $z - 7 = -1$

3. $s + 4 = 10$

4. $8 = a + 4$

5. $5 = 1 + b$

6. $-5 = k - 8$

7. $s - 2 = 0$

8. $m + 6 = 11$

9. $12 = 2 + x$

10. $7 = 3 + z$

11. $-1 = 3 - x$

12. $-7 = k - 10$

13. $0 = 5 - m$

14. $4 = a - 1$

15. $y - 6 = 0$

16. $10 = a + 8$

17. $12 = 7 + a$

18. $z - 4 = -2$

19. $-6 = 3 - m$

20. $10 = s + 7$

21. $4 - a = -4$

22. $k - 5 = 2$

23. $3 = 10 - m$

24. $20 = 10 + z$

25. $10 + b = 19$

26. $1 = y - 7$

27. $k + 6 = 9$

28. $3 - b = 2$

29. $k + 8 = 16$

30. $-1 = x - 10$

31. $m - 8 = 0$

32. $a + 5 = 11$

33. $m - 10 = -4$

34. $13 = 4 + y$

35. $3 = 7 - k$

36. $9 = 2 + a$

37. $10 - k = 4$

38. $-5 = 5 - y$

39. $b + 6 = 13$

40. $14 = 8 + m$

41. $3 - x = -4$

42. $y - 6 = -4$

43. $k + 5 = 13$

44. $0 = 10 - s$

45. $15 = m + 6$

46. $b + 1 = 3$

47. $5 = 6 - a$

48. $0 = a - 3$

49. $6 + a = 15$

50. $x + 1 = 9$

51. $9 = 10 - z$

52. $7 - x = -1$

53. $1 = 7 - m$

54. $11 = 2 + m$

Solving Inequalities

1.

$8 < y - {-8}$

2.

$7 > 7 + y$

3.

$2 > 9 + z$

4.

$6 < 1 - x$

5.

$$9 \leq m - 5$$

6.

$$5 \leq z + -2$$

7.

$$6 \leq -2 - k$$

8.

$$6 + x \geq 9$$

9.

$3 \leq 2 + x$

10.

$x - {-6} < 2$

11.

$4 > -3 + k$

12.

$6 \leq -8 - x$

13.

$$-5 < y + -8$$

14.

$$5 < x - -5$$

15.

$$9 < z - 1$$

16.

$$1 \geq y + -8$$

17. $8 + k \geq 7$

18. $3 - y > 9$

19. $5 < m - \text{-}8$

20. $\text{-}5 + x \geq \text{-}2$

Proportional Relationship

Solve each Ratio and Proportion.

1. $\dfrac{2}{} = \dfrac{4}{8}$

2. $\dfrac{9}{} = \dfrac{36}{40}$

3. $\dfrac{3}{4} = \dfrac{}{12}$

4. $\dfrac{1}{3} = \dfrac{5}{}$

5. $\dfrac{5}{7} = \dfrac{}{49}$

6. $\dfrac{4}{6} = \dfrac{40}{}$

7. $\dfrac{3}{} = \dfrac{27}{108}$

8. $\dfrac{6}{10} = \dfrac{60}{}$

9. $\dfrac{1}{9} = \dfrac{7}{}$

10. $\dfrac{3}{5} = \dfrac{}{45}$

11. $\dfrac{1}{2} = \dfrac{}{16}$

12. $\dfrac{5}{} = \dfrac{40}{64}$

13. $\dfrac{}{11} = \dfrac{21}{77}$

14. $\dfrac{3}{5} = \dfrac{12}{}$

15. $\dfrac{}{7} = \dfrac{40}{70}$

16. $\dfrac{3}{} = \dfrac{12}{40}$

17. $\dfrac{8}{9} = \dfrac{}{18}$

18. $\dfrac{3}{} = \dfrac{9}{18}$

19. $\dfrac{}{2} = \dfrac{10}{20}$

20. $\dfrac{2}{} = \dfrac{6}{12}$

21. $\dfrac{}{12} = \dfrac{45}{60}$

22. $\dfrac{1}{8} = \dfrac{2}{}$

23. $\dfrac{}{11} = \dfrac{27}{33}$

24. $\dfrac{2}{} = \dfrac{14}{21}$

25. $\dfrac{7}{} = \dfrac{56}{72}$

26. $\dfrac{1}{5} = \dfrac{2}{}$

27. $\dfrac{1}{} = \dfrac{6}{72}$

28. $\dfrac{4}{10} = \dfrac{24}{}$

29. $\dfrac{1}{4} = \dfrac{}{28}$

30. $\dfrac{1}{3} = \dfrac{}{24}$

31. $\dfrac{3}{7} = \dfrac{}{70}$

32. $\dfrac{}{2} = \dfrac{4}{8}$

Percentage

Find the percentage of given numbers and percent values.

1. 70% of ☐ = 560

2. 8% of ☐ = 56

3. 4% of ☐ = 24

4. ☐ of 800 = 160

5. ☐ of 500 = 45

6. 90% of 200 = ☐

7. ☐ of 900 = 540

8. 5% of 300 = ☐

9. 15% of 500 = ☐

10. ☐ of 500 = 200

11. 3% of 100 = ☐

12. 300% of 300 = ☐

13. 6% of ☐ = 42

14. 30% of 600 = ☐

15. 25% of 100 = ☐

16. 35% of ☐ = 210

17. ☐ of 300 = 12

18. 2% of ☐ = 10

19. ☐ of 500 = 400

20. 90% of ☐ = 810

21. 30% of ☐ = 60

22. 70% of 500 = ☐

23. 6% of 500 = ☐

24. ☐ of 600 = 54

25. 75% of 600 = ☐

26. 60% of ☐ = 300

27. ☐ of 400 = 32

28. ☐ of 100 = 5

29. 7% of 10 = ☐

30. 100% of 200 = ☐

31. ☐ of 600 = 1200

32. 40% of 300 = ☐

33. 50% of ☐ = 250

34. ☐ of 600 = 60

Convert Percent and Decimals

1. 61 % = ___________________

2. 67 % = ___________________

3. 42 % = ___________________

4. 30 % = ___________________

5. 73 % = ___________________

6. 100 % = ___________________

7. 38 % = ___________________

8. 20 % = ___________________

9. 1 % = ___________________

10. 26 % = ___________________

11. 0.15 = ___________

12. 84 % = ___________

13. 0.44 = ___________

14. 0.23 = ___________

15. 48 % = ___________

16. 45 % = ___________

17. 60 % = ___________

18. 0.78 = ___________

19. 51 % = ___________

20. 14 % = ___________

21. 0.8 = ___________

22. 52 % = ___________

23. 0.47 = ________________

24. 59 % = ________________

25. 0.94 = ________________

26. 28 % = ________________

27. 0.39 = ________________

28. 0.82 = ________________

29. 0.04 = ________________

30. 65 % = ________________

31. 0.29 = ________________

32. 86 % = ________________

33. 13 % = ________________

34. 90 % = ________________

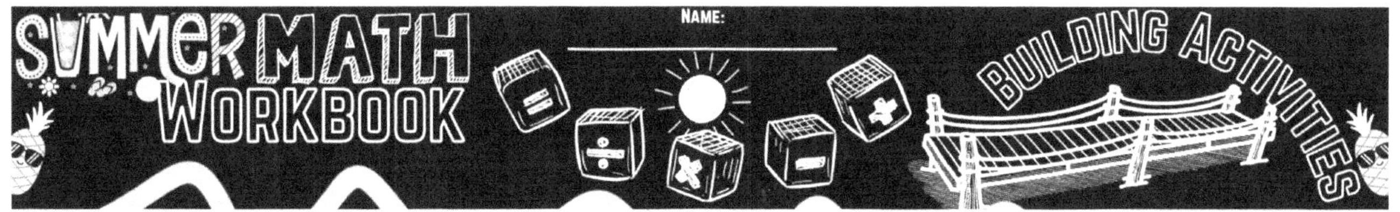

Convert: Ratio, Fraction, Percent, and Decimals

1.

	Ratio	Fraction	Percent	Decimal
a.			70.6%	
b.				0.2
c.	6:12			
d.		10/15		
e.	2:7			
f.	13:15			
g.		8/11		
h.		19/20		
i.	2:2			
j.		2/20		
k.		8/14		
l.		11/17		
m.	1:2			
n.		3/11		
o.			92.9%	

2.

	Ratio	Fraction	Percent	Decimal
a.	10:11			
b.		1/2		
c.		13/15		
d.		3/5		
e.				0.333
f.	2:2			
g.	4:16			
h.	8:9			
i.			73.7%	
j.			37.5%	
k.	10:18			
l.	2:12			
m.		7/13		
n.			75%	
o.	1:4			

3.

	Ratio	Fraction	Percent	Decimal
a.				0.889
b.	3:20			
c.		3/18		
d.				0.526
e.			20%	
f.	16:17			
g.	9:12			
h.	7:7			
i.				0.273
j.	11:20			
k.				0.167
l.		6/20		
m.	9:14			
n.		2/17		
o.	10:14			

Area and Perimeter

1.

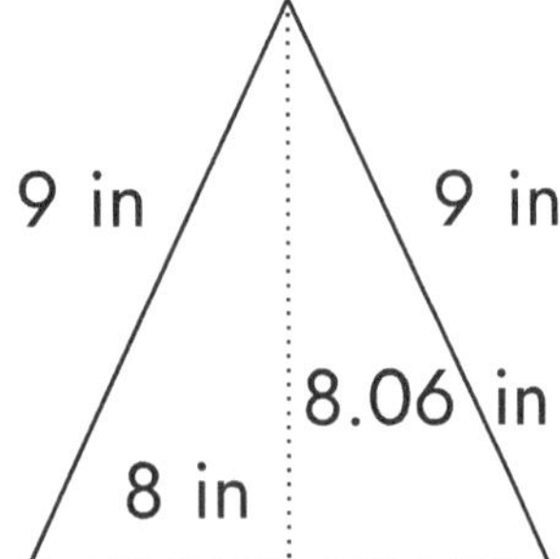

2.

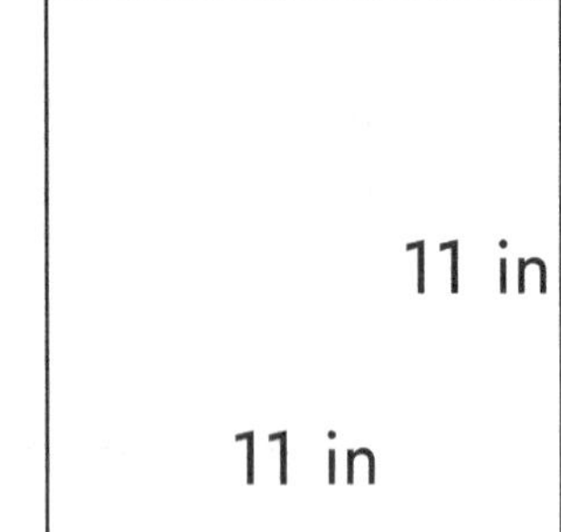

3.

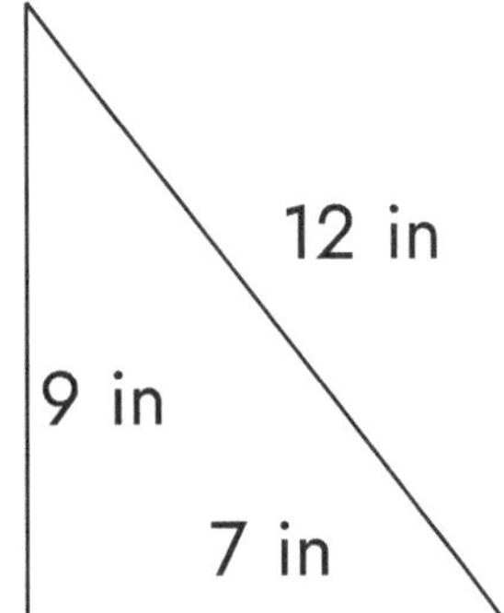

4.

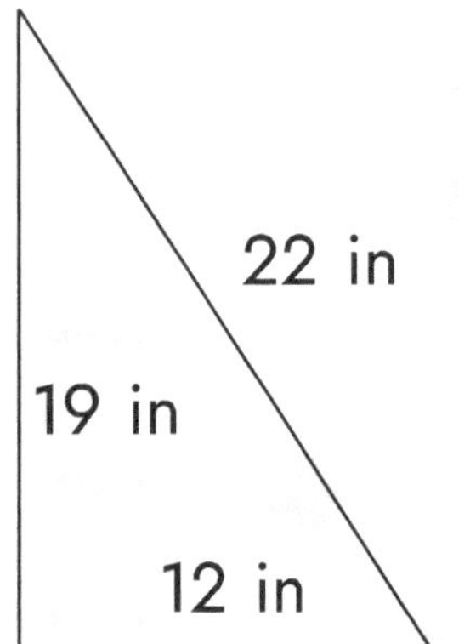

SUMMER MATH WORKBOOK
NAME:
BUILDING ACTIVITIES

5.

10 in
10 in
8.660 in
10 in

6.

3 in
5 in
2.88 in
6 in

7.

5 in
12 in
6 in
14 in

8.

10 in
10 in
8.660 in
10 in

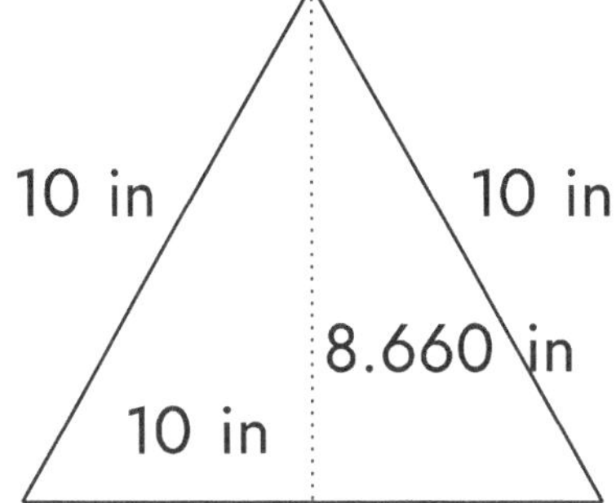

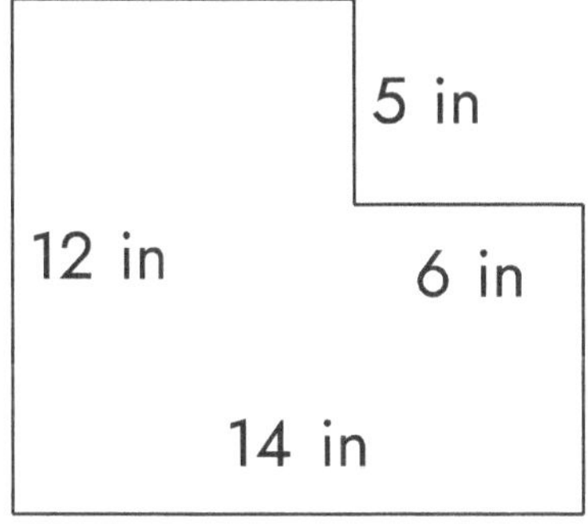

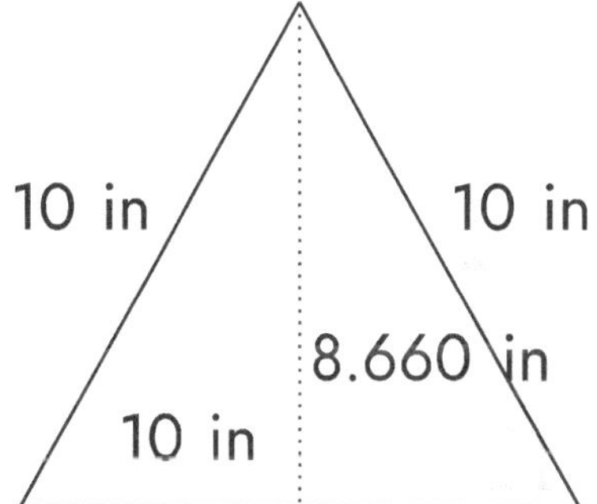

SUMMER MATH
WORKBOOK
NAME:
BUILDING ACTIVITIES

9.

14 in
14 in
12.124 in
14 in

10.

4 in
5 in
7 in
5 in

11.

14 in
9 in
10 in

12.

9 in
5 in
10 in

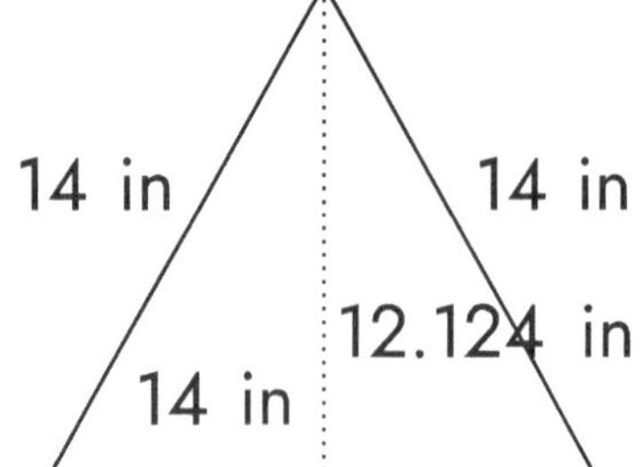

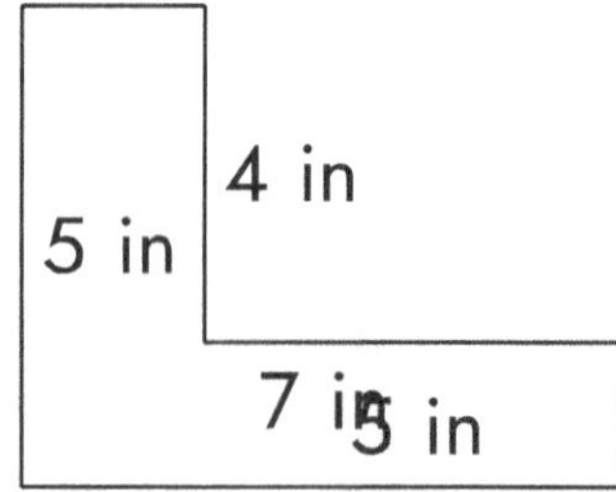

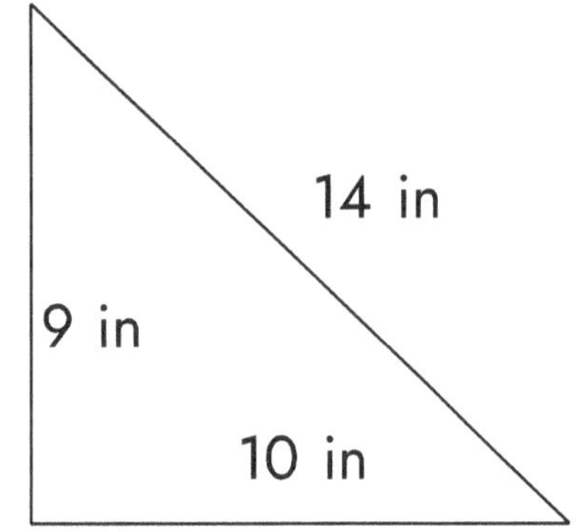

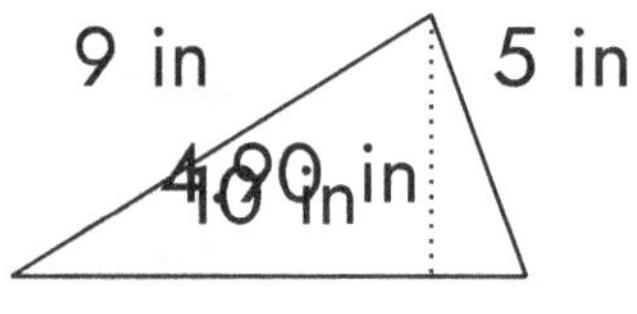

13.

12 in
12 in
11.31 in
8 in

14.

5 in
5 in
5 in
4.330 in

15.

19 in
13 in
14 in

16.

8 in
5 in

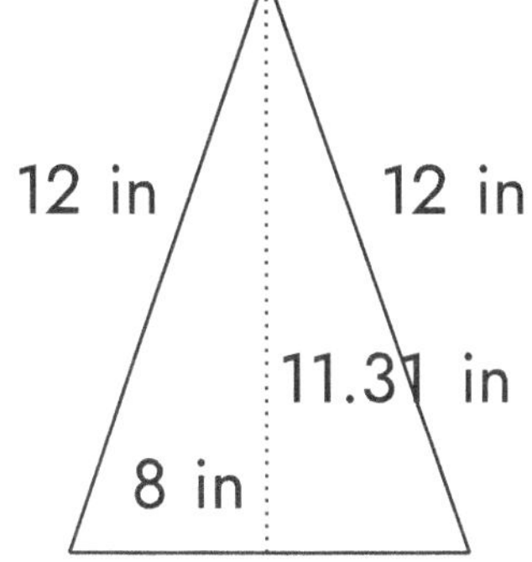

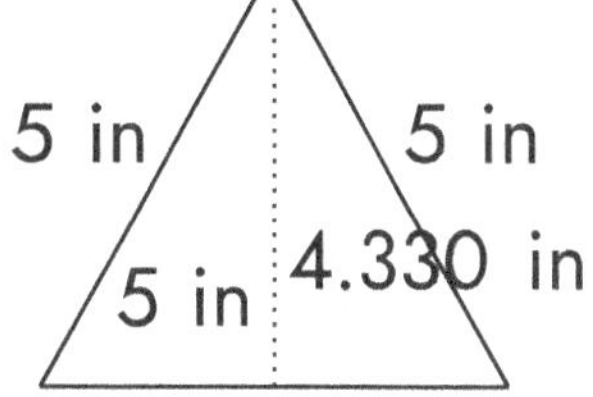

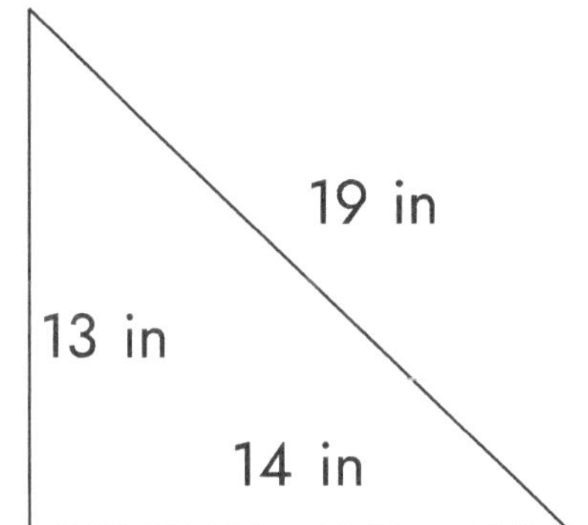

17.

14 in

10 in

18.

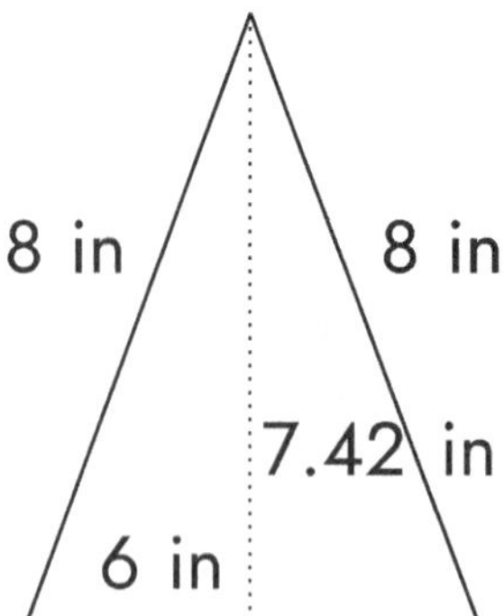

8 in

8 in

7.42 in

6 in

19.

11 in

14 in

20.

12 in

12 in

SUMMER MATH WORKBOOK
NAME:
BUILDING ACTIVITIES

21.

8 in
4 in
7 in
4 in

22.

22 in
19 in
11 in

23.

9 in
9 in
7.794 in
9 in

24.

8 in
5 in
4.32 in

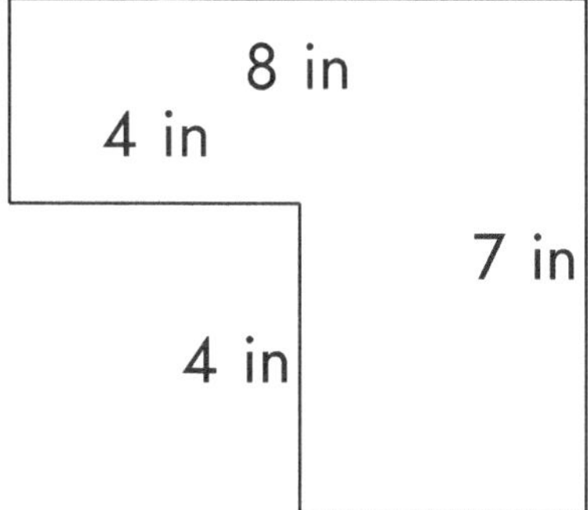

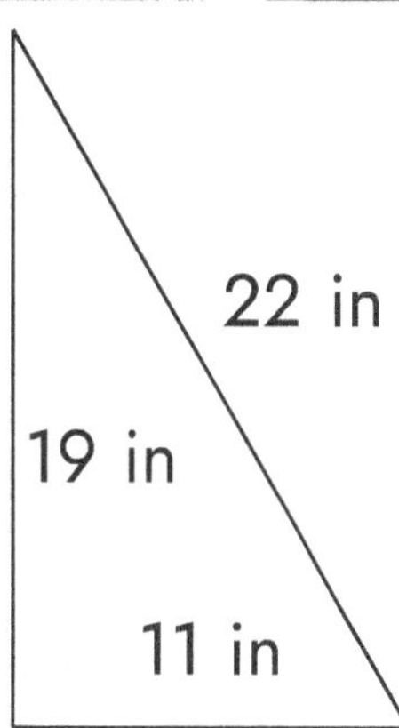

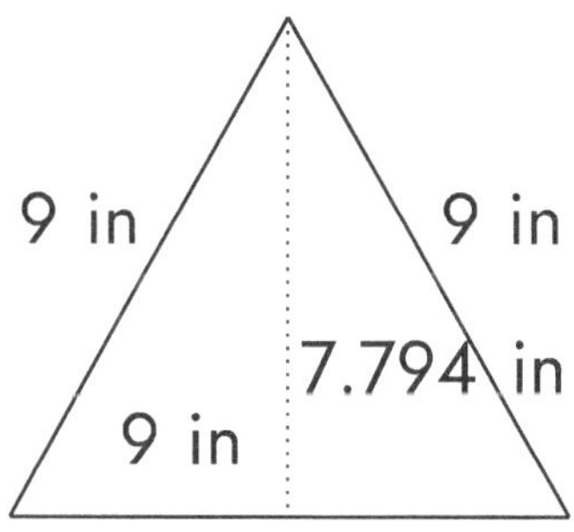

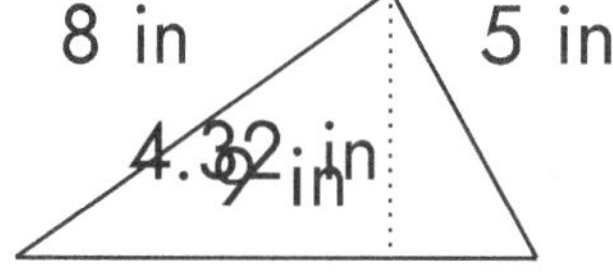

25.

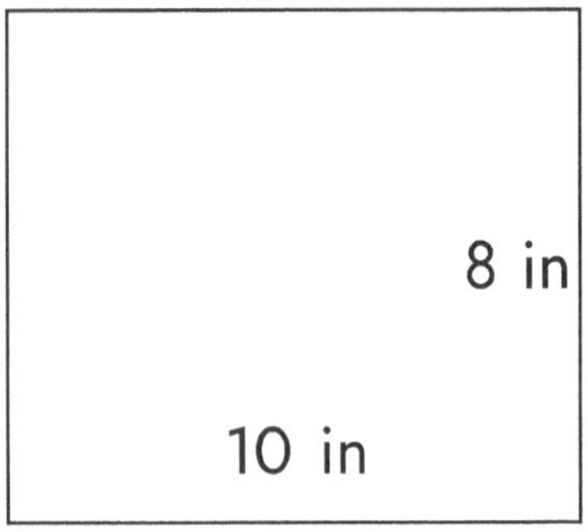

8 in
10 in

26.

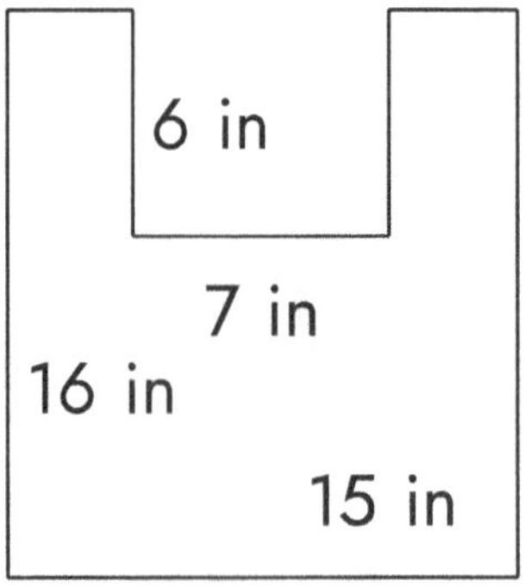

6 in
7 in
16 in
15 in

27.

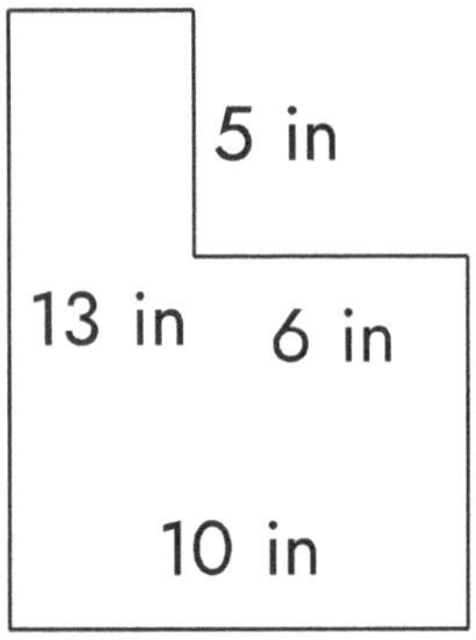

5 in
13 in
6 in
10 in

28.

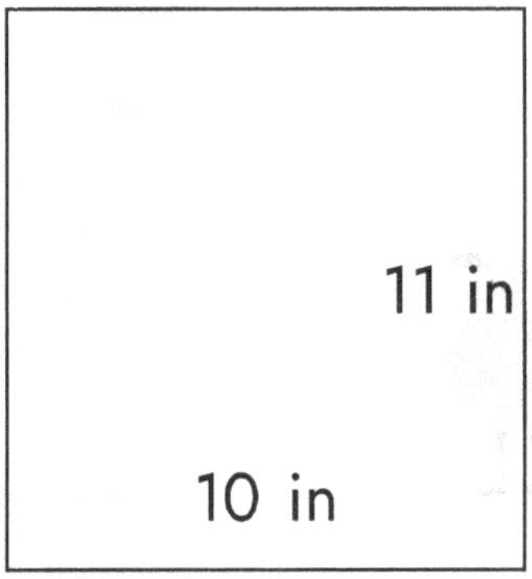

11 in
10 in

Classify and Measure Angles

1.

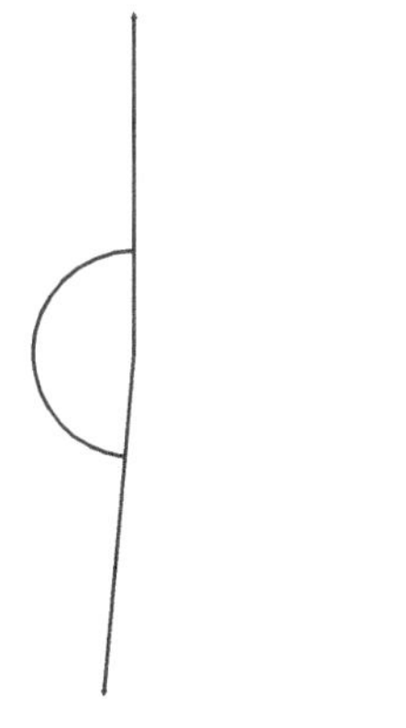

2.

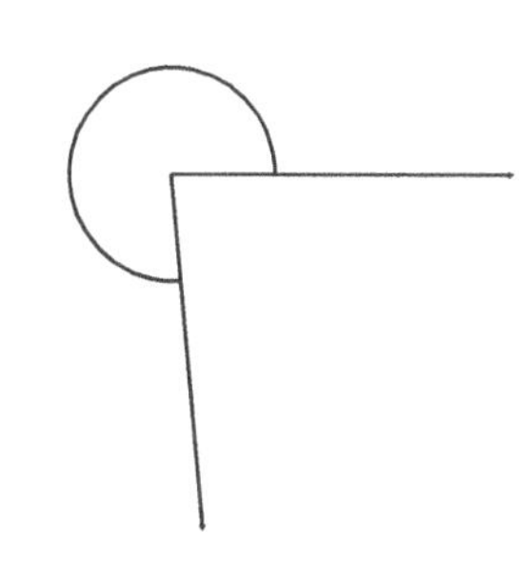

3.

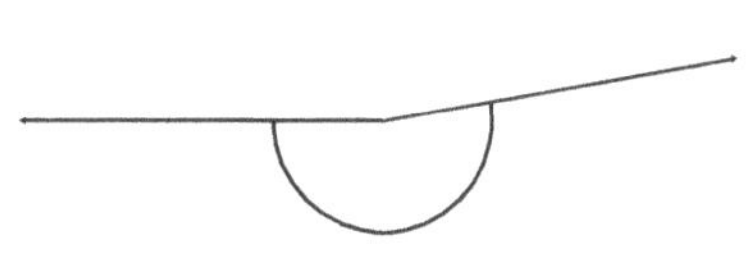

4.

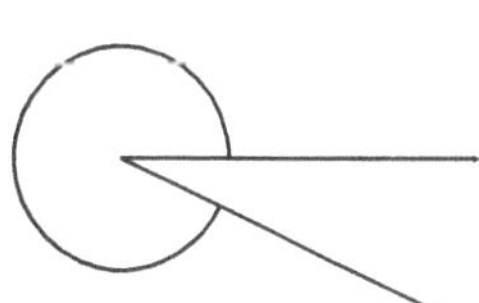

5.

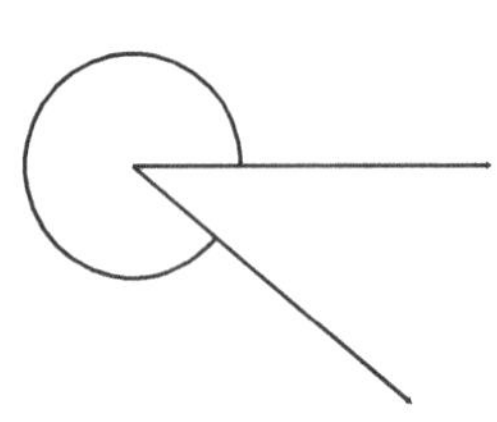

____

6.

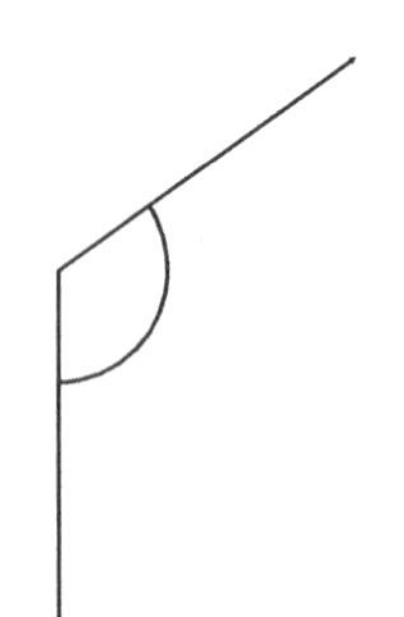

____

7.

____

8.

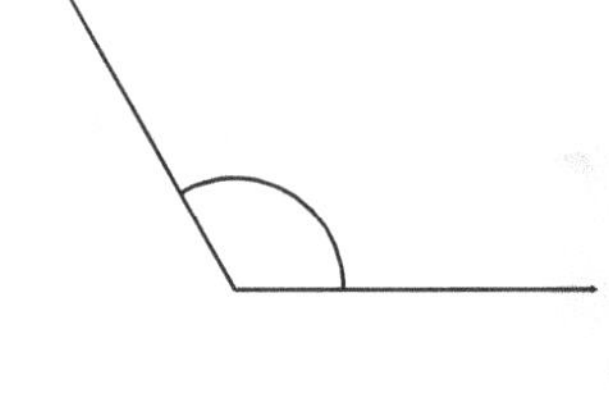

____

9.

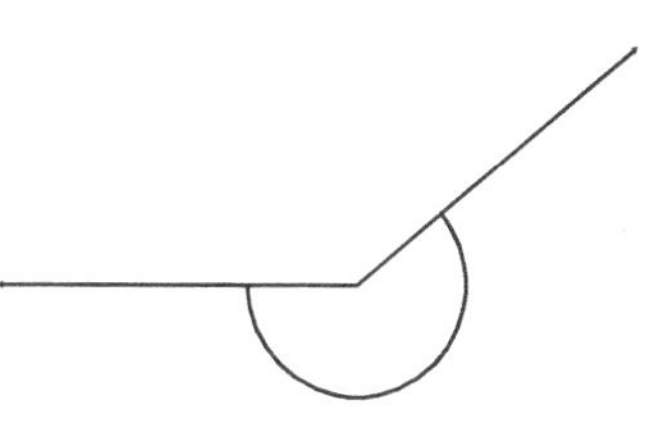

____

10.

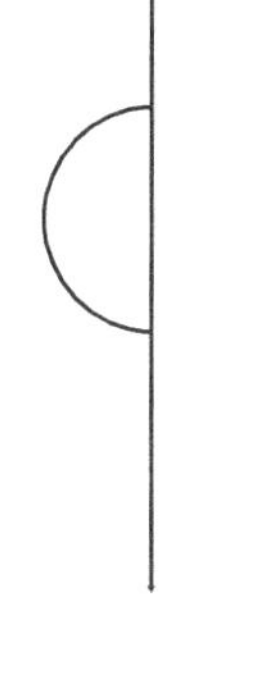

____

11.

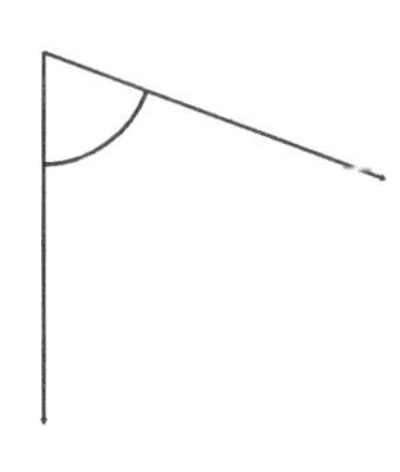

____

12.

____

13.

____

14.

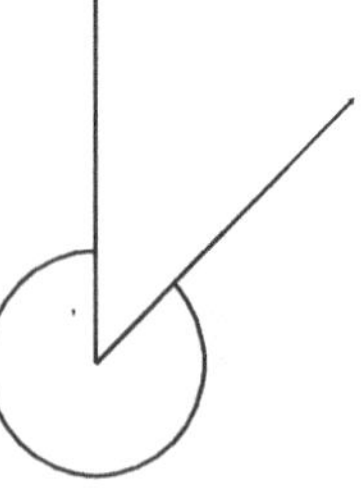

____

15.

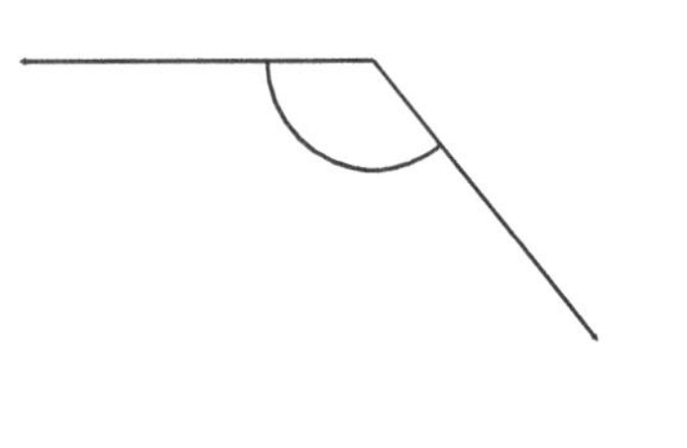

____

16.

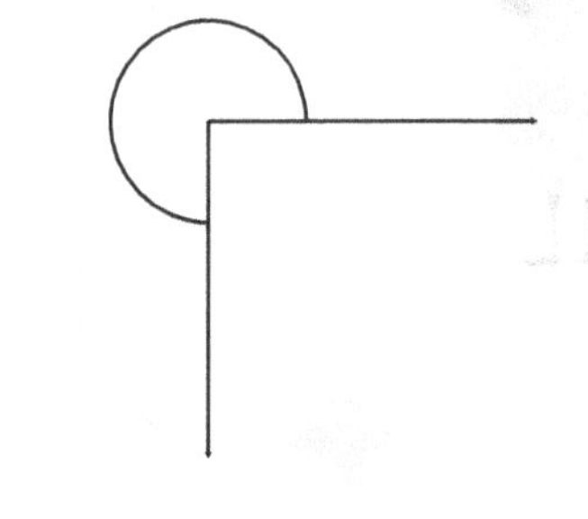

____

17.

____

18.

____

19.

____

20.

____

21.

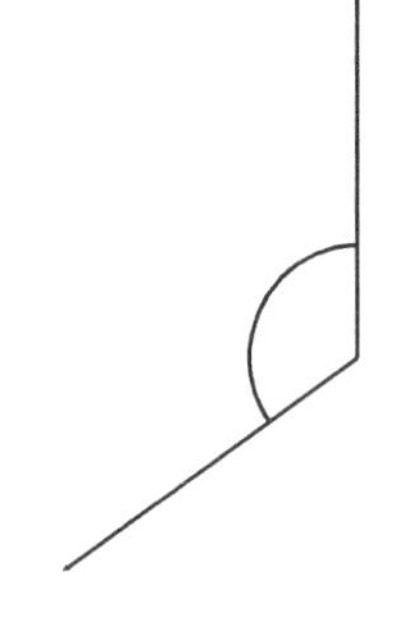

____

22.

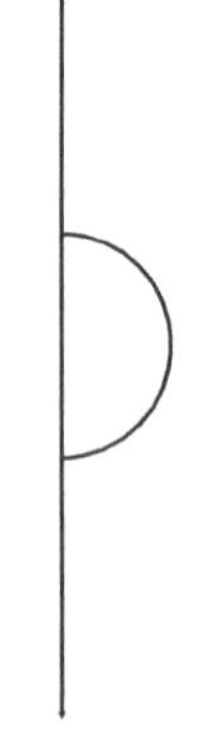

____

23.

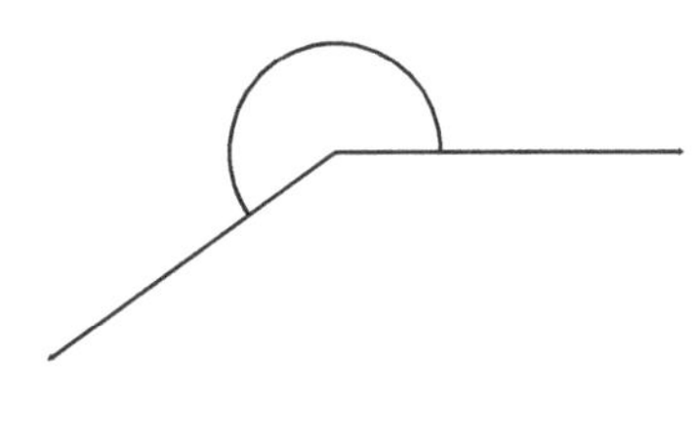

____

24.

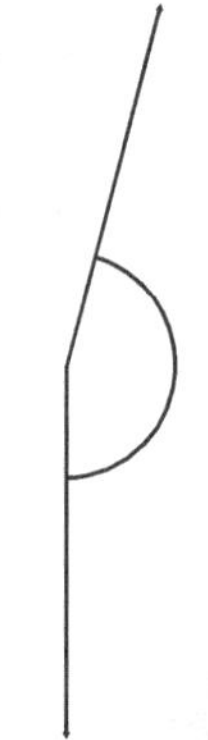

____

Volume and Surface Area

1. 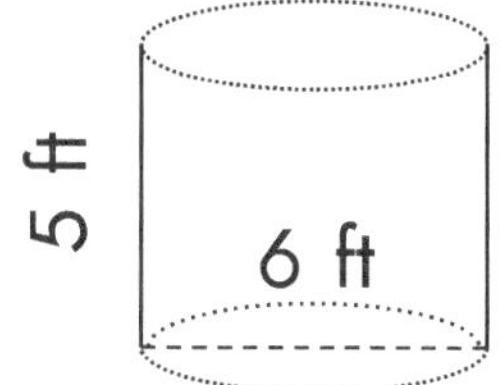

2. 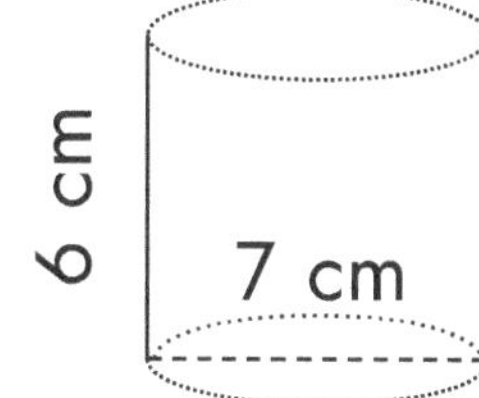

3. 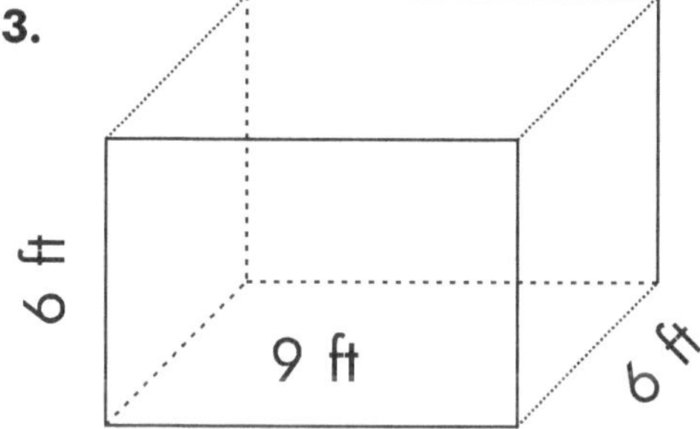

4. 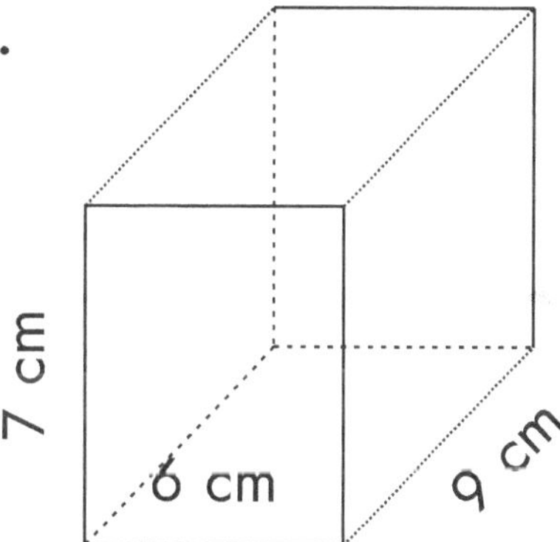

5.

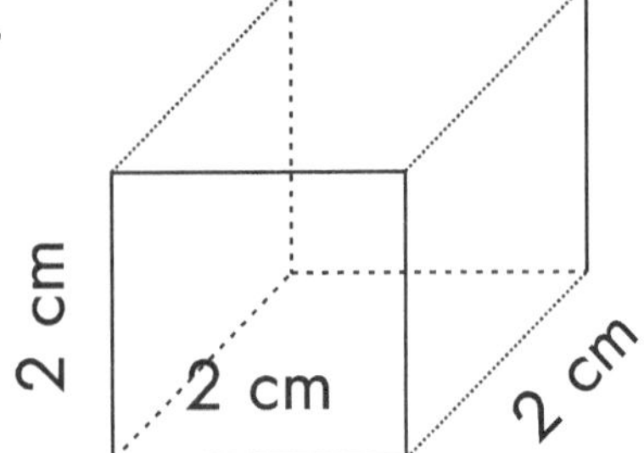

6.

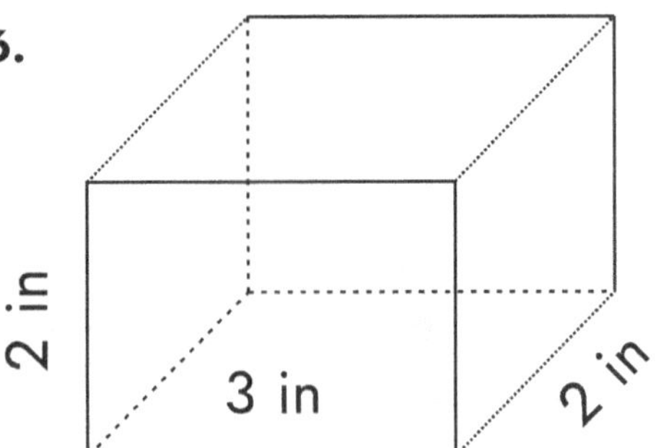

7.

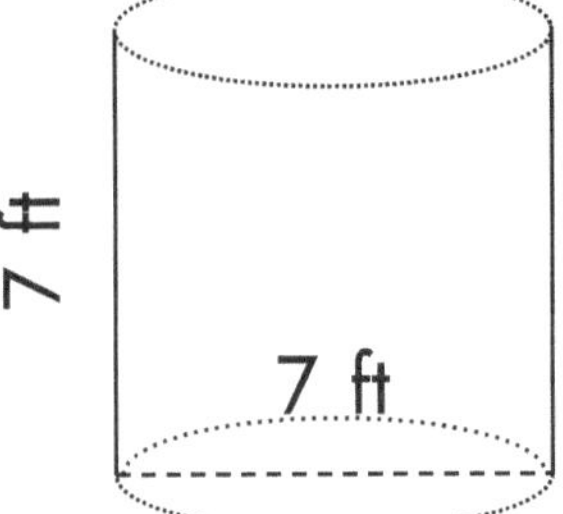

8.

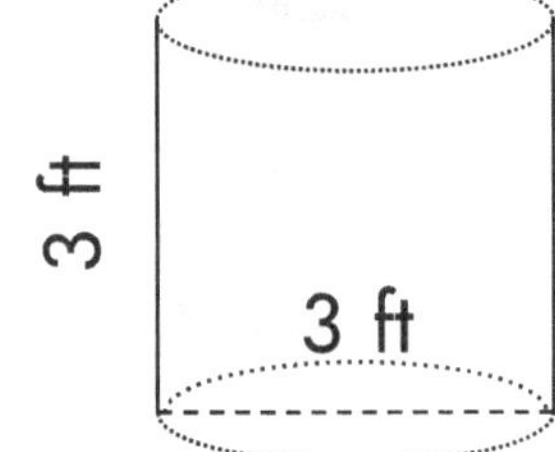

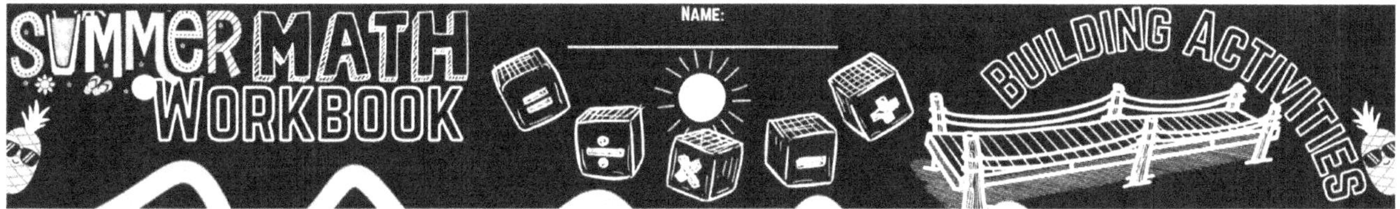

9.

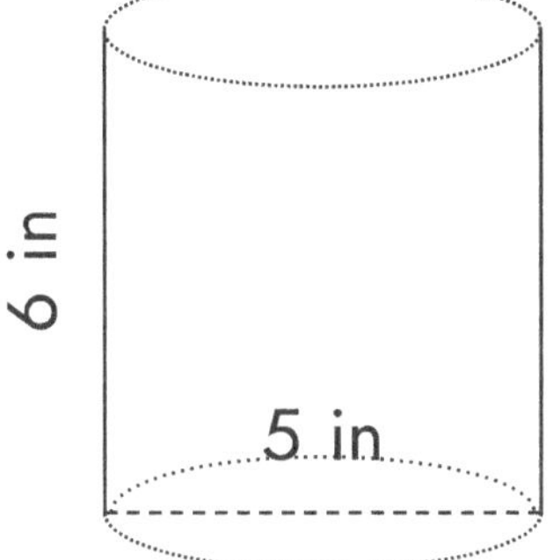

10.

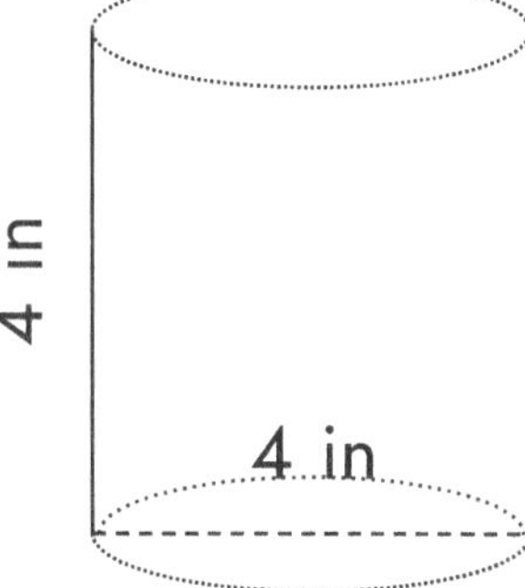

11.

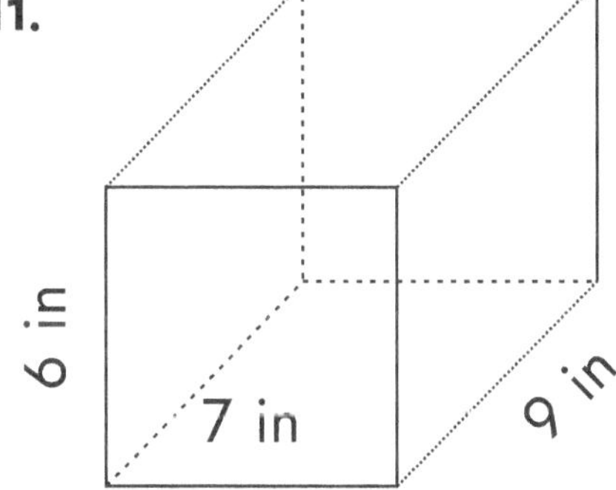

12.

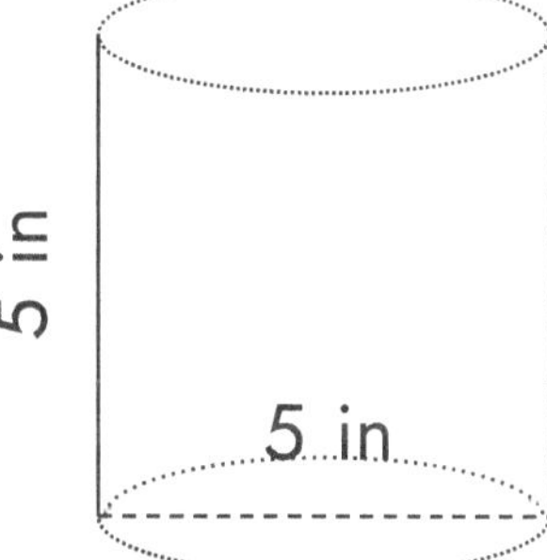

13.

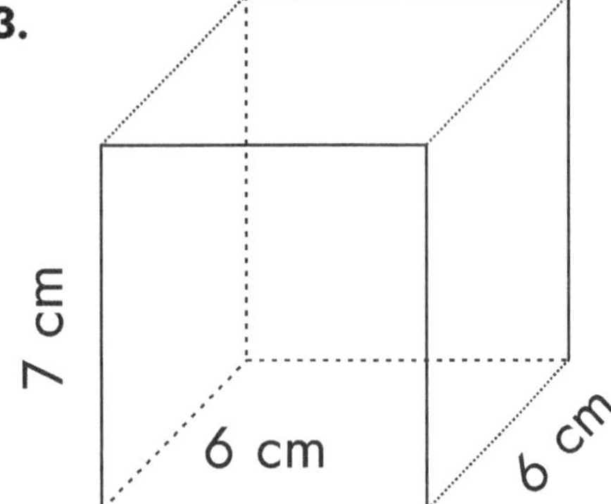

14.

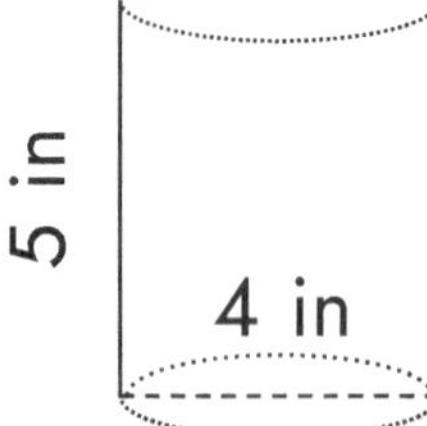

15.

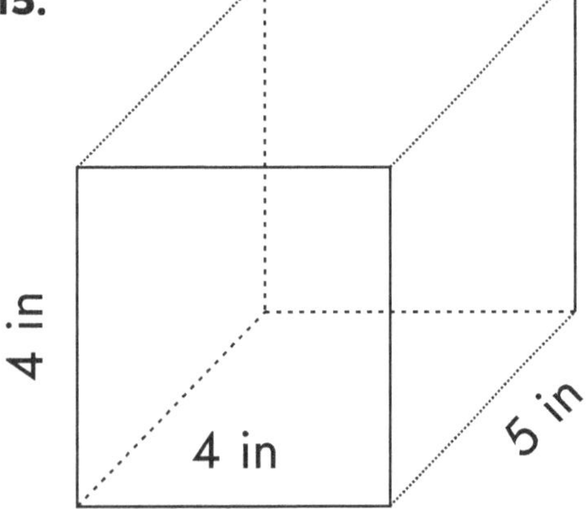

16.

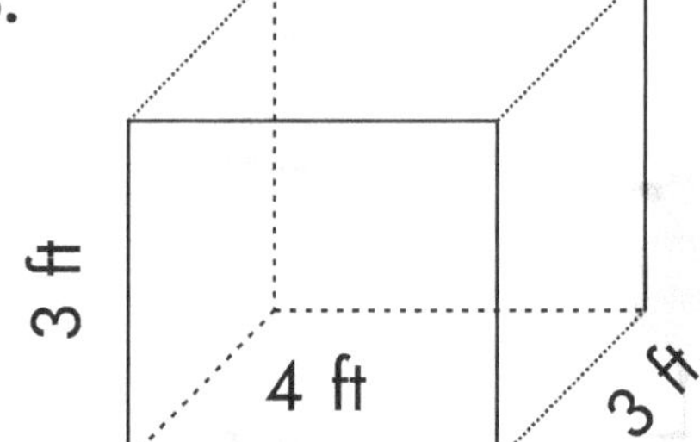

SUMMER MATH WORKBOOK
NAME:
BUILDING ACTIVITIES

17.

3 in
4 in
4 in

18.

5 in
7 in
5 in

19.

4 cm
6 cm

20.

7 in
10 in
10 in

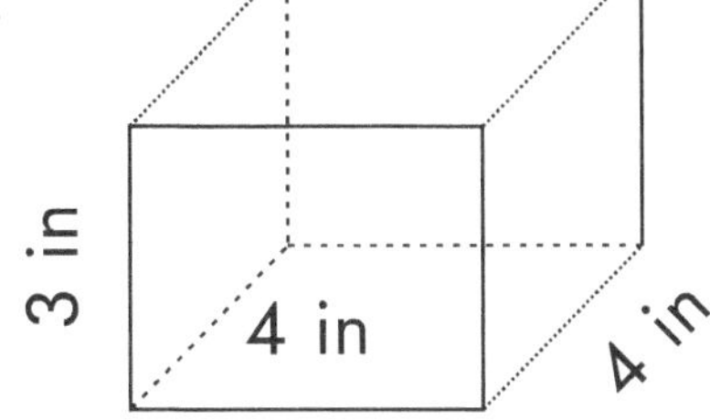

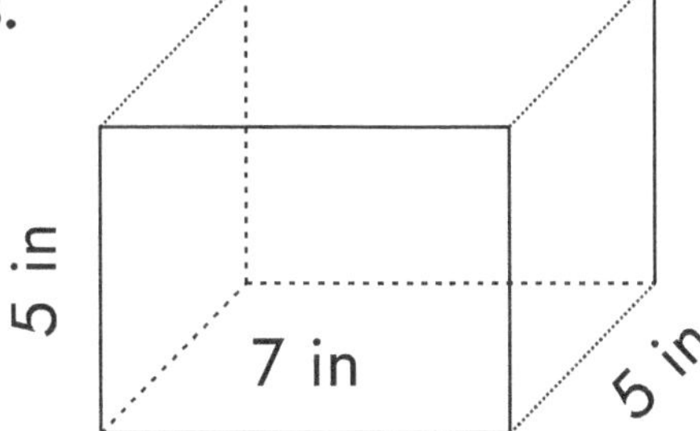

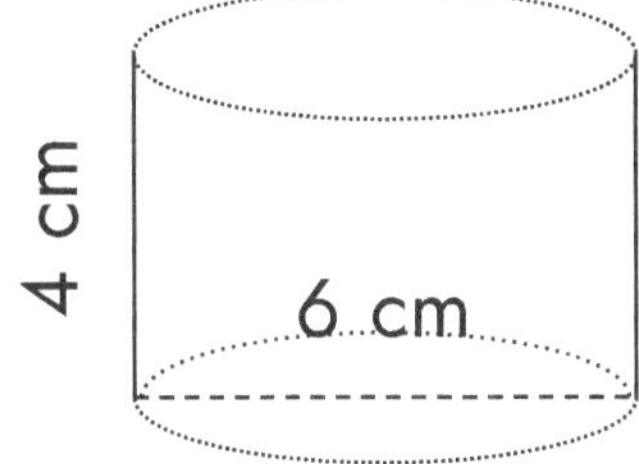

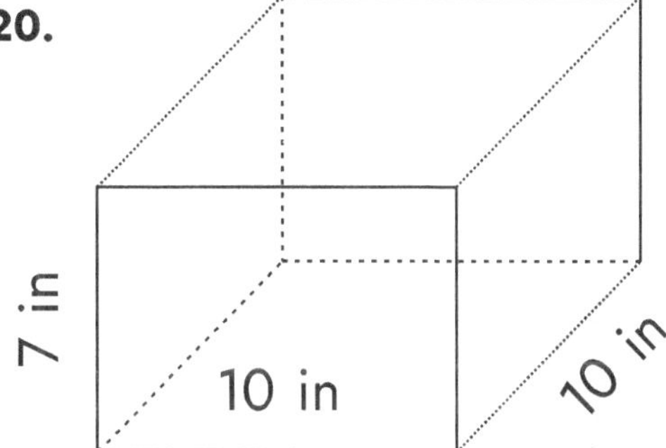

SUMMER MATH WORKBOOK
NAME:
BUILDING ACTIVITIES

21.

6 in
8 in
7 in

22.

3 cm
6 cm

23.

4 in
3 in

24.

6 in
8 in
6 in

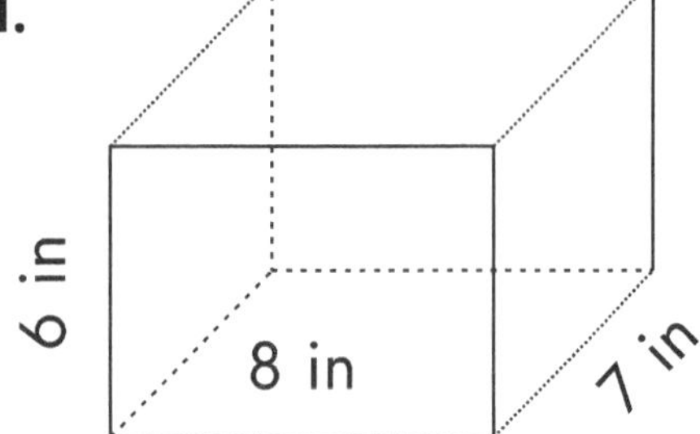

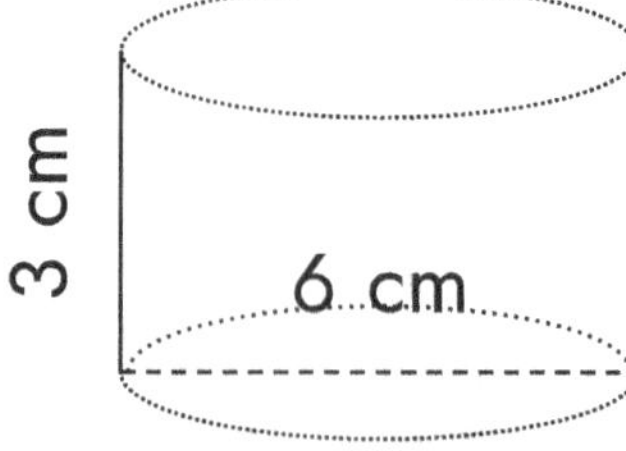

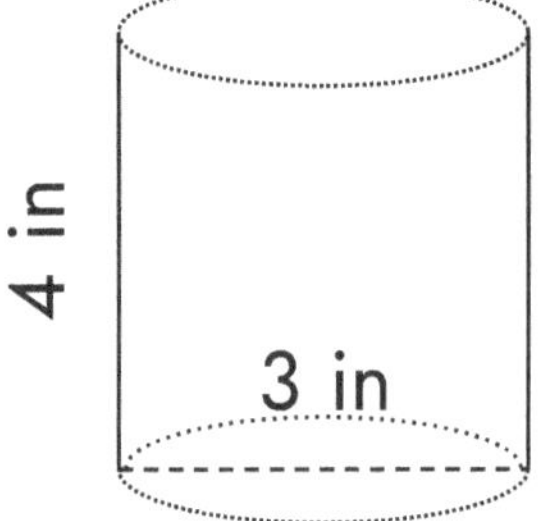

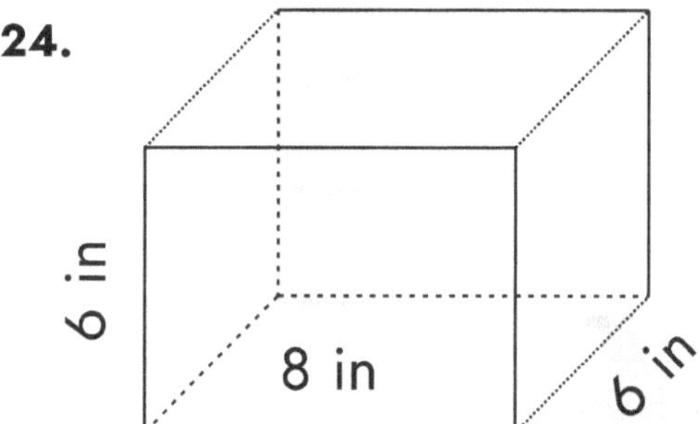

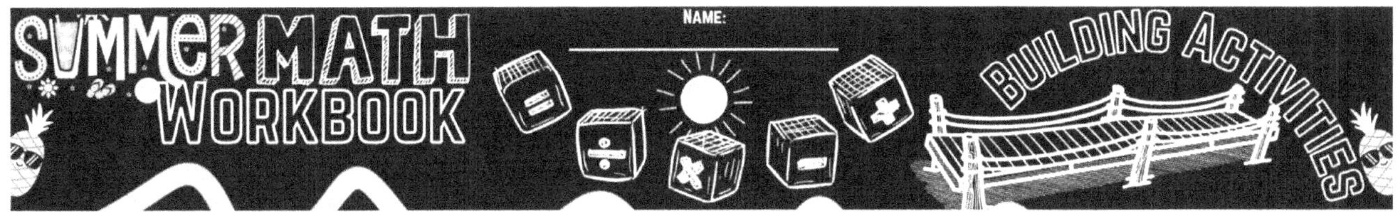

25.

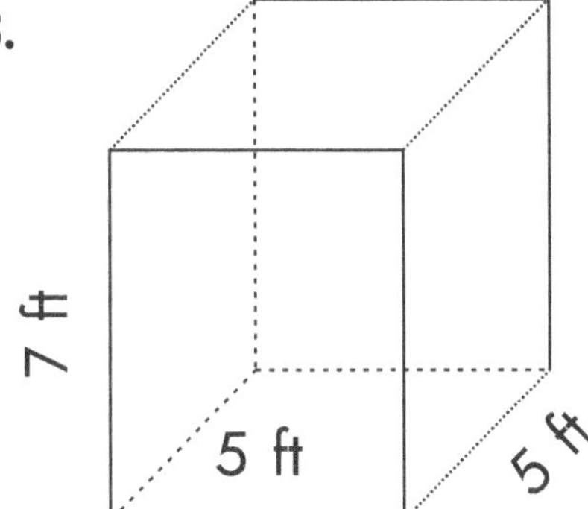

26.

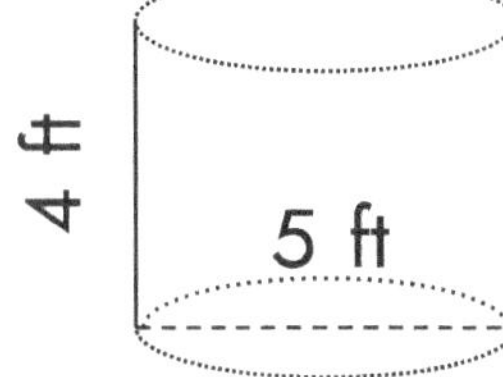

27.

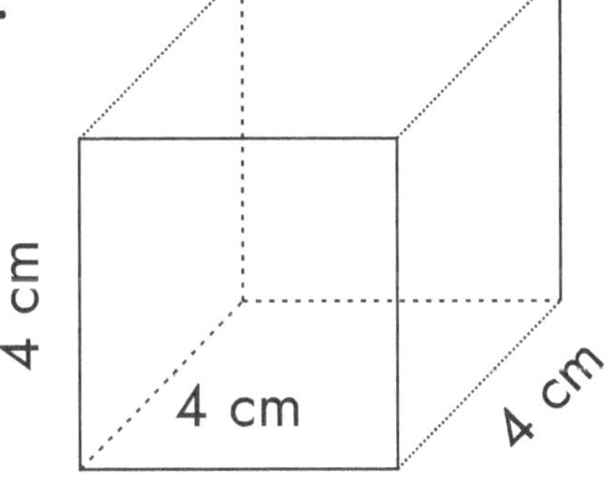

28.

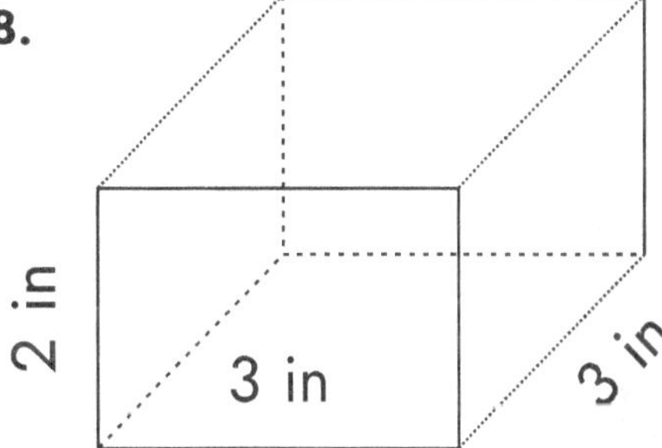

29.

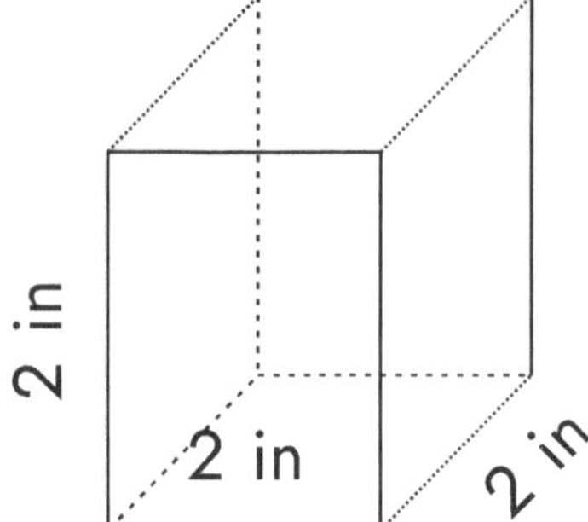

30.

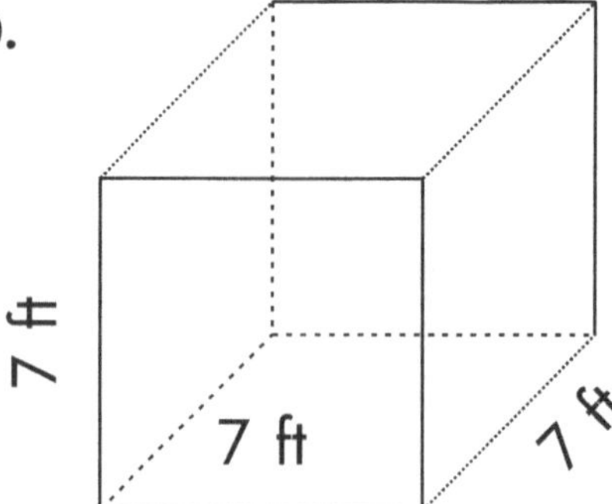

31.

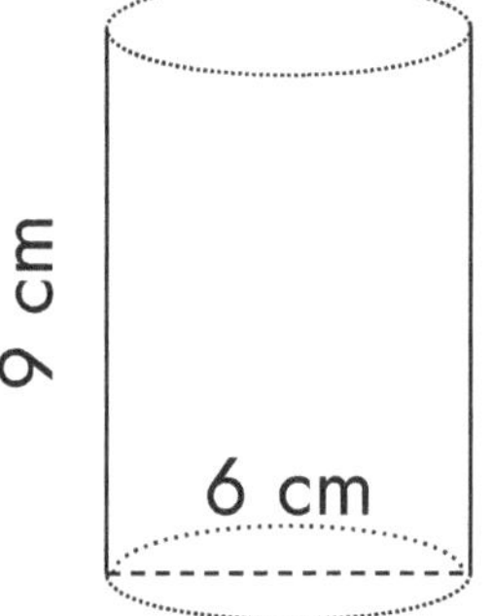

32.

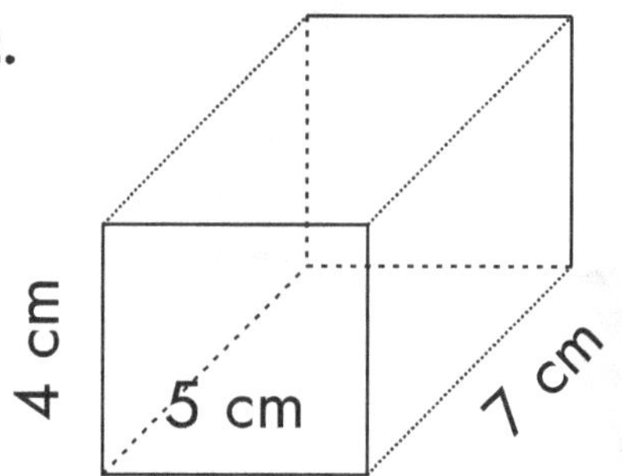

Mean, Median, Mode, and Range

Find the Mean, Median, Mode and Range of the following sets of data.

1. 72, 73, 50, 16, 9, 67, 91

   Mean = _____   Median = _____

   Mode = _____   Range = _____

2. 67, 28, 35, 76, 30, 57, 26

   Mean = _____   Median = _____

   Mode = _____   Range = _____

3. 83, 31, 97, 90, 36, 27, 64

   Mean = _____   Median = _____

   Mode = _____   Range = _____

4. 74, 1, 65, 55, 14, 37, 97

Mean = _____   Median = _____

Mode = _____   Range = _____

5. 13, 7, 42, 47, 52, 67

Mean = _____   Median = _____

Mode = _____   Range = _____

6. 53, 42, 38, 83, 42, 91

Mean = _____   Median = _____

Mode = _____   Range = _____

7. 26, 24, 75, 80, 33, 3

Mean = _____   Median = _____

Mode = _____   Range = _____

8. 36, 84, 55, 60, 24, 11, 43

Mean = _______   Median = _____

Mode = _______   Range = _____

9. 82, 61, 98, 72, 85, 61, 94

Mean = _____   Median = _____

Mode = _____   Range = _____

10. 30, 93, 55, 22, 93, 30

Mean = _______   Median = _____

Mode = _______   Range = _____

11. 77, 89, 73, 42, 93, 14

Mean = _______   Median = _____

Mode = _______   Range = _____

12. 49, 45, 2, 41, 99, 21, 32

Mean = _______   Median = _____

Mode = _______   Range = _____

13. 52, 78, 53, 43, 52, 82

Mean = _____   Median = _____

Mode = _____   Range = _____

14. 32, 5, 69, 7, 54, 69, 53

Mean = _______   Median = _____

Mode = _______   Range = _____

15. 23, 47, 61, 33, 68, 53

Mean = _____   Median = _____

Mode = _____   Range = _____

16. 87, 4, 25, 46, 11, 13, 67

Mean = _______   Median = _______

Mode = _______   Range = _______

17. 11, 61, 98, 81, 21, 99

Mean = _______   Median = _______

Mode = _______   Range = _______

18. 52, 53, 9, 17, 77, 50

Mean = _______   Median = _______

Mode = _______   Range = _______

19. 3, 39, 61, 25, 8, 83

Mean = _______   Median = _______

Mode = _______   Range = _______

20.   19, 72, 41, 90, 3, 83

Mean = _______   Median = _____

Mode = _______   Range = _____

21.   68, 72, 46, 33, 29, 28

Mean = _____   Median = _____

Mode = _____   Range = _____

22.   32, 42, 30, 85, 72, 70

Mean = _______   Median = _____

Mode = _______   Range = _____

23.   6, 88, 86, 54, 17, 99

Mean = _______   Median = _____

Mode = _______   Range = _____

ANSWERS

Page 1:   Exponents

1. 25 **2.** 1/100 **3.** 1/169 **4.** 1/361 **5.** 729 **6.** 27

7. 1/121 **8.** 1,296 **9.** 4,096 **10.** 3,375 **11.** 1/256 **12.** 2,744

13. 1/25 **14.** 16 **15.** 1/36 **16.** 1/8000 **17.** 1/144 **18.** 4,096

19. 1/216 **20.** 6,561 **21.** 1/4913 **22.** 343 **23.** 1/16 **24.** 1/6859

25. 2,197 **26.** 36 **27.** 81 **28.** 400 **29.** 5,832 **30.** 361

Page 4:   Square and Cube Roots

1. 13 **2.** 1 **3.** 6 **4.** 31 **5.** 3 **6.** 12 **7.** 10 **8.** 5 **9.** 8

10. 5 **11.** 32 **12.** 17 **13.** 4 **14.** 1 **15.** 8 **16.** 22 **17.** 14 **18.** 21

19. 2 **20.** 9 **21.** 12 **22.** 2 **23.** 23 **24.** 15 **25.** 7 **26.** 19 **27.** 20

28. 7 **29.** 16 **30.** 28 **31.** 25 **32.** 46 **33.** 24 **34.** 63 **35.** 10 **36.** 9

Page 7:   Factors

1. 2, 4 **2.** 3, 11 **3.** 2, 3, 4, 6

4. 2, 5 **5.** None **6.** 3, 31

7. 2, 3, 5, 6, 10, 15 **8.** None **9.** None

10. 3, 7 **11.** 2, 3 **12.** 2, 19

13. 7, 11 **14.** None **15.** 3, 7, 9, 21

16. None **17.** None **18.** None

19. 2 **20.** 5 **21.** 2, 4, 19, 38

22. 3, 9 **23.** None **24.** None

25. 5, 13   **26.** 2, 29   **27.** None

28. 2, 4, 8, 16, 32

Page 11: Multiples

1. 11, 22, 33, 44, 55

2. 31, 62, 93, 124, 155

3. 3, 6, 9, 12, 15

4. 5, 10, 15, 20, 25

5. 6, 12, 18, 24, 30

6. 9, 18, 27, 36, 45

7. 94, 188, 282, 376, 470

8. 46, 92, 138, 184, 230

9. 4, 8, 12, 16, 20

10. 59, 118, 177, 236, 295

11. 2, 4, 6, 8, 10

12. 8, 16, 24, 32, 40

13. 100, 200, 300, 400, 500

14. 65, 130, 195, 260, 325

15. 75, 150, 225, 300, 375

16. 26, 52, 78, 104, 130

17. 69, 138, 207, 276, 345

18. 56, 112, 168, 224, 280

19. 93, 186, 279, 372, 465

20. 73, 146, 219, 292, 365

21. 60, 120, 180, 240, 300

22. 80, 160, 240, 320, 400

23. 96, 192, 288, 384, 480

24. 43, 86, 129, 172, 215

25. 44, 88, 132, 176, 220

26. 52, 104, 156, 208, 260

27. 1, 2, 3, 4, 5

28. 71, 142, 213, 284, 355

Page 15: Positive and Negative Integers

1. 15   **2.** 20   **3.** 26   **4.** 25   **5.** 17   **6.** 21   **7.** 21   **8.** 8   **9.** 20

10. 21   **11.** 17   **12.** 26   **13.** 14   **14.** 20   **15.** 16   **16.** 12   **17.** 23   **18.** 24

19. 14   **20.** 14   **21.** 20   **22.** 12   **23.** 19   **24.** 11   **25.** 25   **26.** 16   **27.** 19

28. 27   **29.** 18   **30.** 22   **31.** 14   **32.** 15   **33.** 18   **34.** 20

Page 22:   Order of Operations (PEMDAS)

1. 29   **2.** 25   **3.** 26   **4.** 9   **5.** 12   **6.** 22   **7.** 21   **8.** 17   **9.** 18

10. 16   **11.** 7   **12.** 18   **13.** 8   **14.** 19   **15.** 20   **16.** 27   **17.** 21   **18.** 25

19. 15   **20.** 13   **21.** 20   **22.** 13   **23.** 10   **24.** 17   **25.** 21   **26.** 22   **27.** 15

28. 14

Page 25:   Solving Equations: (One Side)

1. $x = 5$ **2.** $x = 11$ **3.** $x = 11$ **4.** $x = 16$ **5.** $x = 65$ **6.** $x = 3$

7. $x = 90$ **8.** $x = 17$ **9.** $x = 20$ **10.** $x = 7$ **11.** $x = 2$ **12.** $x = 14$

13. $x = 17$ **14.** $x = 12$ **15.** $x = 6$ **16.** $x = 2$ **17.** $x = 10$ **18.** $x = 20$

19. $x = 4$ **20.** $x = 3$ **21.** $x = 18$ **22.** $x = 2$ **23.** $x = 5$ **24.** $x = 26$

25. $x = 8$ **26.** $x = 13$ **27.** $x = 3$ **28.** $x = 14$

Page 28:   Evaluate Expressions

1. -7   **2.** 7   **3.** 7   **4.** 0   **5.** 10   **6.** 9   **7.** -8   **8.** 3

Page 29:   Evaluate Expressions

1. 11   **2.** -1   **3.** 5   **4.** 14   **5.** 3   **6.** 1   **7.** -3   **8.** 9

Page 30:   Evaluate Expressions

1. -4   **2.** -7   **3.** -8   **4.** 5   **5.** 4   **6.** 0   **7.** -2   **8.** 11

Page 31:   Evaluate Expressions

1. 12   **2.** -1   **3.** -1   **4.** 0   **5.** 5   **6.** 11   **7.** 3   **8.** -2

Page 32:   One-Step Equations

1. 5   **2.** 6   **3.** 6   **4.** 4   **5.** 4   **6.** 3   **7.** 2   **8.** 5   **9.** 10

10. 4   **11.** 4   **12.** 3   **13.** 5   **14.** 5   **15.** 6   **16.** 2   **17.** 5   **18.** 2

19. 9   **20.** 3   **21.** 8   **22.** 7   **23.** 7   **24.** 10   **25.** 9   **26.** 8   **27.** 3

28. 1   **29.** 8   **30.** 9   **31.** 8   **32.** 6   **33.** 6   **34.** 9   **35.** 4   **36.** 7

37. 6   **38.** 10   **39.** 7   **40.** 6   **41.** 7   **42.** 2   **43.** 8   **44.** 10   **45.** 9

46. 2   **47.** 1   **48.** 3   **49.** 9   **50.** 8   **51.** 1   **52.** 8   **53.** 6   **54.** 9

Page 39: Solving Inequalities

1. $y > 0$ **2.** $y < 0$ **3.** $z < -7$ **4.** $x < -5$ **5.** $m \geq 14$ **6.** $z \geq 7$

7. $k \leq -8$ **8.** $x \geq 3$ **9.** $x \geq 1$ **10.** $x < -4$ **11.** $k < 7$ **12.** $x \leq -14$

13. $y > 3$ **14.** $x > 0$ **15.** $z > 10$ **16.** $y \leq 9$ **17.** $k \geq -1$ **18.** $y < -6$

19. $m > -3$ **20.** $x \geq 3$

Page 44: Proportional Relationship

1. 4   **2.** 10   **3.** 9   **4.** 15   **5.** 35   **6.** 60   **7.** 12   **8.** 100   **9.** 63

10. 27   **11.** 8   **12.** 8   **13.** 3   **14.** 20   **15.** 4   **16.** 10   **17.** 16   **18.** 6

19. 1   **20.** 4   **21.** 9   **22.** 16   **23.** 9   **24.** 3   **25.** 9   **26.** 10   **27.** 12

28. 60   **29.** 7   **30.** 8   **31.** 30   **32.** 1

Page 47: Percentage

1. 800   **2.** 700   **3.** 600   **4.** 20%   **5.** 9%   **6.** 180   **7.** 60%

8. 15   **9.** 75   **10.** 40%   **11.** 3   **12.** 900   **13.** 700   **14.** 180

15. 25   **16.** 600   **17.** 4%   **18.** 500   **19.** 80%   **20.** 900   **21.** 200

22. 350   **23.** 30   **24.** 9%   **25.** 450   **26.** 500   **27.** 8%   **28.** 5%

29. 0.7   **30.** 200   **31.** 200%   **32.** 120   **33.** 500   **34.** 10%

Page 50: Convert Percent and Decimals

1. 0.61   **2.** 0.67   **3.** 0.42   **4.** 0.3   **5.** 0.73   **6.** 1   **7.** 0.38

8. 0.2   **9.** 0.01   **10.** 0.26   **11.** 15%   **12.** 0.84   **13.** 44%   **14.** 23%

15. 0.48 **16.** 0.45 **17.** 0.6 **18.** 78% **19.** 0.51 **20.** 0.14 **21.** 80%

22. 0.52 **23.** 47% **24.** 0.59 **25.** 94% **26.** 0.28 **27.** 39% **28.** 82%

29. 4% **30.** 0.65 **31.** 29% **32.** 0.86 **33.** 0.13 **34.** 0.9

Page 53:   Convert: Ratio, Fraction, Percent, and Decimals

1.

	Ratio	Fraction	Percent	Decimal
a.	12:17	12/17	70.6%	0.706
b.	2:10	2/10	20%	0.2
c.	6:12	6/12	50%	0.5
d.	10:15	10/15	66.7%	0.667
e.	2:7	2/7	28.6%	0.286
f.	13:15	13/15	86.7%	0.867
g.	8:11	8/11	72.7%	0.727
h.	19:20	19/20	95%	0.95
i.	2:2	2/2	100%	1
j.	2:20	2/20	10%	0.1
k.	8:14	8/14	57.1%	0.571
l.	11:17	11/17	64.7%	0.647
m.	1:2	1/2	50%	0.5
n.	3:11	3/11	27.3%	0.273
o.	13:14	13/14	92.9%	0.929

2.

	Ratio	Fraction	Percent	Decimal
a.	10:11	10/11	90.9%	0.909
b.	1:2	1/2	50%	0.5
c.	13:15	13/15	86.7%	0.867
d.	3:5	3/5	60%	0.6
e.	4:12	4/12	33.3%	0.333
f.	2:2	2/2	100%	1
g.	4:16	4/16	25%	0.25
h.	8:9	8/9	88.9%	0.889
i.	14:19	14/19	73.7%	0.737
j.	3:8	3/8	37.5%	0.375
k.	10:18	10/18	55.6%	0.556
l.	2:12	2/12	16.7%	0.167
m.	7:13	7/13	53.8%	0.538
n.	3:4	3/4	75%	0.75
o.	1:4	1/4	25%	0.25

3.

	Ratio	Fraction	Percent	Decimal
a.	16:18	16/18	88.9%	0.889
b.	3:20	3/20	15%	0.15
c.	3:18	3/18	16.7%	0.167
d.	10:19	10/19	52.6%	0.526
e.	1:5	1/5	20%	0.2
f.	16:17	16/17	94.1%	0.941
g.	9:12	9/12	75%	0.75
h.	7:7	7/7	100%	1
i.	3:11	3/11	27.3%	0.273
j.	11:20	11/20	55%	0.55
k.	1:6	1/6	16.7%	0.167
l.	6:20	6/20	30%	0.3
m.	9:14	9/14	64.3%	0.643
n.	2:17	2/17	11.8%	0.118
o.	10:14	10/14	71.4%	0.714

Page 56:   Area and Perimeter

1. P=26 A=32.24
2. P=44 A=121
3. P=28 A=31.5

4. P=53 A=114
5. P=30 A=43.3
6. P=14 A=8.64

7. P=52 A=138
8. P=30 A=43.3
9. P=42 A=84.87

10. P=24 A=15
11. P=33 A=45
12. P=24 A=24.5

13. P=32 A=45.24
14. P=15 A=10.82
15. P=46 A=91

16. P=26 A=40
17. P=48 A=140
18. P=22 A=22.26

19. P=50 A=154
20. P=48 A=144
21. P=30 A=40

22. P=52 A=104.5
23. P=27 A=35.07
24. P=22 A=19.44

25. P=36 A=80
26. P=74 A=198
27. P=46 A=100

28. P=42 A=110

Page 63:   Classify and Measure Angles

1. 175° Obtuse   **2.** 275° Reflex   **3.** 190° Reflex   **4.** 335° Reflex

5. 320° Reflex   **6.** 125° Obtuse   **7.** 65° Acute   **8.** 120° Obtuse

9. 220° Reflex   **10.** 180° Straight   **11.** 70° Acute   **12.** 45° Acute

13. 165° Obtuse   **14.** 315° Reflex   **15.** 130° Obtuse   **16.** 270° Reflex

17. 140° Obtuse   **18.** 115° Obtuse   **19.** 230° Reflex   **20.** 50° Acute

21. 125° Obtuse   **22.** 180° Straight   **23.** 215° Reflex   **24.** 165° Obtuse

Page 69:   Volume and Surface Area

1. V=141.37 ft³ ft³ SA=151 ft² ft²

2. V=230.91 cm³ cm³ SA=209 cm² cm²

3. V=324 ft³ ft³ SA=288 ft² ft²

4. V=378 cm³ cm³ SA=318 cm² cm²

5. V=8 cm³ cm³ SA=24 cm² cm²

6. V=12 in³ in³ SA=32 in² in²

7. V=269.39 ft³ ft³ SA=231 ft² ft²

8. V=21.21 ft³ ft³ SA=42 ft² ft²

9. V=117.81 in³ in³ SA=134 in² in²

10. V=50.27 in³ in³ SA=75 in² in²

11. V=378 in³ in³ SA=318 in² in²

12. V=98.17 in³ in³ SA=118 in² in²

13. V=252 cm³ cm³ SA=240 cm² cm²

14. V=62.83 in³ in³ SA=88 in² in²

15. V=80 in³ in³ SA=112 in² in²

16. V=36 ft³ ft³ SA=66 ft² ft²

17. V=48 in³ in³ SA=80 in² in²

18. V=175 in³ in³ SA=190 in² in²

19. V=113.10 cm³ cm³ SA=132 cm² cm²

20. V=700 in³ in³ SA=480 in² in²

21. V=336 in³ in³ SA=292 in² in²

22. V=84.82 cm³ cm³ SA=113 cm² cm²

23. V=28.27 in³ in³ SA=52 in² in²

24. V=288 in³ in³ SA=264 in² in²

25. V=175 ft³ ft³ SA=190 ft² ft²

26. V=78.54 ft³ ft³ SA=102 ft² ft²

27. V=64 cm³ cm³ SA=96 cm² cm²

28. V=18 in³ in³ SA=42 in² in²

29. V=8 in³ in³ SA=24 in² in²

30. V=343 ft³ ft³ SA=294 ft² ft²

31. V=254.47 cm³ cm³ SA=226 cm² cm²

32. V=140 cm³ cm³ SA=166 cm² cm²

Page 77: Mean, Median, Mode, and Range

1. Mean = 54, Median = 67, Mode = none, Range = 82

2. Mean = 45.571, Median = 35, Mode = none, Range = 50

3. Mean = 61.143, Median = 64, Mode = none, Range = 70

4. Mean = 49, Median = 55, Mode = none, Range = 96

5. Mean = 38, Median = 44.5, Mode = none, Range = 60

6. Mean = 58.167, Median = 47.5, Mode = 42, Range = 53

7. Mean = 40.167, Median = 29.5, Mode = none, Range = 77

8. Mean = 44.714, Median = 43, Mode = none, Range = 73

9. Mean = 79, Median = 82, Mode = 61, Range = 37

10. Mean = 53.833, Median = 42.5, Mode = 30, 93, Range = 71

11. Mean = 64.667, Median = 75, Mode = none, Range = 79

12. Mean = 41.286, Median = 41, Mode = none, Range = 97

13. Mean = 60, Median = 52.5, Mode = 52, Range = 39

14. Mean = 41.286, Median = 53, Mode = 69, Range = 64

15. Mean = 47.5, Median = 50, Mode = none, Range = 45

16. Mean = 36.143, Median = 25, Mode = none, Range = 83

17. Mean = 61.833, Median = 71, Mode = none, Range = 88

18. Mean = 43, Median = 51, Mode = none, Range = 68

19. Mean = 36.5, Median = 32, Mode = none, Range = 80

20. Mean = 51.333, Median = 56.5, Mode = none, Range = 87

21. Mean = 46, Median = 39.5, Mode = none, Range = 44

22. Mean = 55.167, Median = 56, Mode = none, Range = 55

23. Mean = 58.333, Median = 70, Mode = none, Range = 93